The Communication Barrier in International Management

Dimitris N. Chorafas

AMA Research Study 100

THE COMMUNICATION BARRIER
IN INTERNATIONAL MANAGEMENT

AMA RESEARCH STUDY 100

THE COMMUNICATION BARRIER IN INTERNATIONAL MANAGEMENT

Dimitris N. Chorafas

AMERICAN MANAGEMENT ASSOCIATION, INC.

This Research Study has been distributed without
charge to AMA members enrolled in the International
Management Division.

Standard book number: 8144–3100–3
Library of Congress catalog card number: 73–98622

About This Report

$\mathbf{M}$ORE THAN ANY OTHER EVENT, the recent moon landing of our astronauts highlights the phenomenal technological strides made during the past few decades. The landing was an incredible feat; and, in the eyes of millions of television viewers, the moon walk was our first real 20th-century adventure. That the viewing public was able to watch the astronauts' activities on the moon was as remarkable as the mission itself.

The 20th century has brought numerous other technological wonders, such as supersonic aircraft, computers, satellite radios, and video-tape recording. The result has been a world made smaller by more rapid transportation and communication, in which information is gathered more easily and disseminated more freely. Because messages can now be sent from continent to continent and from country to country with ease, many persons assume that communication from man to man can also be accomplished with ease.

As the present report indicates, this assumption should not be made too hastily. Man has broken the sound barrier and has crossed many hurdles, but he has not yet learned to overcome the greatest barrier of all—his limited ability to exchange ideas with his fellow man. He tends to be shortsighted, resistant to unfamiliar concepts, skeptical, and on occasion irrational. These reactions are intensified by distances, language and cultural differences, economic variables, and many other factors.

International corporations are especially susceptible to communication problems. In many firms, the headquarters executives lack field experience in other countries and the overseas executives lack corporate-level experience. Executives in the field maintain that, as a consequence, headquarters executives frequently tend to underestimate the importance of country-by-country differences, request more information than necessary, and impose inapplicable policies and procedures. Headquarters officials maintain that executives in international subsidiaries and divisions tend to over-emphasize the importance of local differences, provide data that are not understandable, and resist wholehearted adoption of methods urged by corporate headquarters. Communications channels between these two groups of executives often become clogged with unnecessary data, rather than being used to relay important information about operational, economic, and political changes. Few international companies have been able to resolve these problems completely, but some have eased them considerably by adopting measures described in this report.

The author, DR. DIMITRIS N. CHORAFAS, graduated from the Sorbonne as a Docteur de l'Université de Paris en Mathématiques. He received an M.S.E. from the University of California at Los Angeles and attended the University of Denver, George Washington University, and the National Technical University in Athens. From 1956 to 1962 he served on the faculty of the School of Engineering and Architecture at the Catholic University of America, and he has also been associated with the University of California, Washington State University, and Georgia Institute of Technology.

Dr. Chorafas was affiliated with Booz, Allen and Hamilton International, Inc., as director-management information systems and since 1961 has had a private consulting practice in Paris. He is the author of 30 books and numerous articles on industrial research, engineering, applied mathematics, electronic computers, and management.

The author acknowledges with thanks the assistance provided in the editing of the manuscript by Margaret V. Higginson, AMA research program director, and Roberta Pavlu, AMA assistant editor.

JOHN W. ENELL
Vice President for Research

Contents

Exhibits

1. The Complexities of International Business Communication

ONE OF THE PREVALENT COM-munication barriers that exist in international management today was described by the general manager of a Latin American subsidiary as follows:

Many of the senior executives who come here are such fast flyers that after they leave we have to write to them and complete the communication. Sometimes one headquarters executive comes in for half the morning, another one comes at noon, and a third in the afternoon. By the time we have thought about what was said, they are already at the airport checking in their luggage.

These quick, random meetings are not enough. They do not allow professional relationships to grow. The best that can be achieved is a merchandiser's relationship, which is seldom personal. The people who come here do not understand our problems, nor do we understand the intricate aspects of policy making at headquarters, no matter how often we read the written policy statements. Yet, there is no question that we would have liked much more personal contact, including the guidance, advice, and perspectives this can bring.

Because such problems are prevalent in international management, the present study was conducted to determine the underlying causes of communication barriers, primarily between international companies and their foreign subsidiaries and affiliates, and to examine the methods these companies use to overcome such barriers. Since major problems spring not so much from outside disturbances as from inside the international company, this report concentrates on discussions with executives of international companies' headquarters and subsidiaries.

In general, the methods described are not highly structured since business communications are not yet smoothly running and closely knit, and policies and practices are still at an early stage of development. The author was somewhat surprised when he did discover that policy guidance on communication was not yet well formulated in the international companies he studied and that they were devoting far less time and effort to communication than he had assumed.

The study was intended to describe approaches taken in overcoming barriers rather than unsuccessful efforts or failures to communicate. Nevertheless, the report is heavily weighted with descriptions of impasses and anxieties. Also, it may seem overly pessimistic because it denies the value of sensible honesty as a means of securing desirable communication, and it lacks success stories about companies that solved their problems by installing well-defined programs. In addition, the report serves as a warning to people of goodwill who assume that most international information problems arise out of "misunderstanding."

This report documents in a factual manner some of the steps that have to be taken by international companies if they are to improve their communication. A few of these steps are as follows:

- Create sound policies to guide communication. Since such policies must be applicable through a company's operations, they must have enough flexibility to cover immediate situations that are characteristic of each country.
- Face communication problems head-on, instead of shying away from them. Most executives working abroad—

whether they are American, English, German, Italian, or French—said that they had great difficulty communicating with headquarters, but subsequently most headquarters executives said that they had no feeling of communication barriers between themselves and the subsidiaries.

- Eliminate communications on minor

Basis of the Research

Information for this study was obtained through lengthy interviews and correspondence with 143 men in 17 countries. Of these participants, 114 were company executives—42 presidents, vice presidents, and other officers; 39 directors and managers; and 33 other members of management—and 29 were consultants, government officials, and academicians. The participants were situated in the following areas of the world:

		No. of Men
North America:	United States	55
	Mexico and Canada	17
Europe:	Great Britain	13
	France and Italy	13
	Switzerland and Germany	13
Latin America:	Panama	12
	Guatemala and Venezuela	12
	San Salvador and others	5
Near East and Africa:		3
		143

These men represented 55 companies in a variety of industries, services, and institutions: accounting, aircraft, automobiles, banking, chemicals, communications, construction, consulting, drugs, education, electrical and electronic equipment, foods, glass, government, instruments, machinery, office equipment and supplies, rubber, tobacco, transportation, and utilities.

The author visited 36 of the participating companies two years ago. He conducted approximately 50 interviews with executives in subsidiaries of these 36 companies—usually in the executives' native language. Subsequently he corresponded with a number of firms to update data obtained earlier and to obtain more detailed information about their practices and procedures. Since the author is a European who has worldwide business experience and has conducted many studies on international management, he was able to bring extensive knowledge and understanding to this report on the present state of the art of international management communication.

subjects, which represent half the paper going through the pipeline. Chopping the deadwood out of communications will sharply alter the cost of information handling, while making an efficient framework possible.

- Improve the quality of communications by critically examining their characteristics, determining their frequency, and studying their impact in terms of end results. Although this may seem obvious, it is rarely practiced since most communications networks grow like wild flowers.
- Make the image of communication reflect the nature and structure of the organization. Senior executives have confirmed that this is more difficult than it sounds. Communication does not follow organizational patterns; in fact, the clash between them is sometimes very apparent. At times, this illusion results in great inefficiencies, especially when companies do not plan and prepare for worldwide expansion.

The Cost of Misinformation

A basic axiom about communication in international companies needs to be stressed at the outset. On the whole, communication should be on a cost/effectiveness basis as much as possible. This can be achieved by lowering fences, opening channels, minimizing paperwork, and keeping messages brief and to the point. It can also be achieved by decentralizing the foreign subsidiaries and evaluating their performance on the basis of profit and loss and ability to meet objectives. Purposeless reporting often gives companies a distorted picture of the progress abroad and leads them to serious miscalculations.

Men seasoned in international business know from experience that people sometimes fight one another not because they misunderstand a situation but because they understand it only too well. This was confirmed by a horde of examples provided by executives in 17 countries. These men indicated that they had done everything possible to inform others about their situations, but they were met with silence, irrelevant responses, and compromises. And, although some of the compromises were consistent and based on sound business principles, they did not necessarily result in greater efficiency.

In each corporate subsidiary that was visited, executives remarked that their subsidiary had its own special needs, demands, and problems. To say that these are only policy or procedural differences would be to deliberately oversimplify the situation. Psychological factors are also important, since they tend to widen the gap between headquarters and the subsidiaries and cloud communications. In many companies that have suffered from ineffectual communication, executives have refused for psychological reasons to be pushed into spending money for new systems or changing procedures—when they could have found very sound policy or procedural reasons for refusing.

Companies that try to control the communications jungle with budgetary tools may find them more of a disadvantage than an advantage, as emphasized by one international executive: "Budgetary strings are proving to be more useful to the meek and the ignorant who want to abide by the rules than to people who are willing to sail close to the wind."

Let nobody be misguided into believing that international companies can solve their communication problems simply by introducing faster methods. Although computers are bound to play a role in the future, they will be subordinate to human imperatives and less radical than was imagined some years ago. International communication problems can be traced back to the days when domestic companies expanded into other countries without proper planning.

Nanoseconds and minichanges are of little value in the present situation. Large changes are needed, and few persons have enough experience and knowledge to be full-fledged authorities on international communication. Large-scale international operations are a recent development. Nevertheless, it is surprising that even now, when some experience has already been accumulated, no generic approaches have been developed.

Of course, some of the accumulated experience has been more destructive than constructive; that is, companies have learned what they should not do rather than what they should do. Thus few guidelines can be drawn from present practices. Communications channels, a basic prerequisite for good management, are seldom examined in international perspectives. For example, not one participating company had a report-request editor or any person assigned to the job of handling the piles of paper characterizing the international enterprise.

In some quarters, leaving the international communications jungle where it stands is considered a suitable means of postponing painful decisions. While many executives admitted that much of the information flowing in their companies' networks is unusable or unnecessary, few of them had the courage to initiate a cleanup. Few multinational companies asked the crucial questions: What is the minimal information needed by headquarters to make sound decisions? What information is needed by men in the field to do an efficient job? And what is the cost/effectiveness of the information that both groups need?

Of the experienced executives interviewed, not one disagreed that international companies must become more imaginative and resourceful in their communications. They expressed opinions that powerful measures are needed to correct the present situation and that the communications network is not the only area in need of radical repair.

Effective executives and communications are mainsprings in international industrial operations, and their development rests on the same management principles. But principles are seldom applied the same way in the subsidiary as they are at headquarters. The differences may not be apparent and they may not be acute; but, when they exist, misunderstanding can easily occur. For this reason, a communications system has to take all viewpoints into account.

The Gap Between Companies and Their Subsidiaries

One of the primary reasons for the wide gap between executives at headquarters and those in the field was explained by Dr. Robert G. Wertheimer, professor of economics, Babson Institute:

Years of work in the various domestic sectors remain the indispensable basis of any international assignment. This form of apprenticeship provides exposure to various domestic activities and relies on typical on-the-job experience.

A few companies hire directly for the international division, but even here the candidate will be trained by the domestic organization. In the very few cases when an applicant is hired directly for the international training program he will be cut off, so to speak, from a potential domestic career should he fail in his foreign assignment. Even with the active principle enforced everywhere that all promotions should come from within, transfers between domestic and international divisions are considered risky. . . .*

An obvious fact is that two-way communication builds experience, and experience is the most reliable means for obtaining results. As every seasoned executive knows, a critical aspect of managerial performance in multinational operations is determination of standards and measurement criteria. Although a number of executives are experienced in establishing performance standards at home, their experience may not be relevant for foreign operations. International measurement criteria are far more elusive.

Not only does distance create distortion; but, in addition, other factors cause difficulties. At this time there are no generally accepted, valid criteria by which effectiveness of international subsidiaries can be measured. Each subsidiary is relatively self-contained; its transactions are usually confined to the local environment and headquarters. Its operations are often considered atypical or special. Even if meaningful criteria are established for foreign subsidiaries, evaluations made with them may be difficult to fit into the corporate picture. Measurements must be compatible so that results can be gauged against a common denominator.

The lack of homogeneity among international subsidiaries makes meaningful comparisons almost impossible. This has an awkward financial corollary. Alberto Stampa, of the secretary general's office of Pirelli, made this point:

The Pirelli group considers the problem of communication and exchange of information within the company a matter of prime importance. Experience has shown that, when communication is inefficiently organized, considerable economic losses result—mainly from the overlapping of work and functions and the waste of time and energy that accompanies it. Unless a company directs its whole effort toward a single, pre-established aim, the organization will suffer.

One of the chief causes of such a state of affairs is poor coordination. The lack of an adequate and efficient network of information and company communications can be attributed to factors of varying nature, the most important of which are organizational. However, different causes—not formally connected with organizational problems but in substance of considerable importance—must not be underestimated.

Despite the presence of modern procedural systems, certain managerial attitudes and mentalities may cause total paralysis and nonapplication. This is clearly a problem of major importance to the company, since its staff members must have understanding and acceptance of the organizational pattern in which they live and work.

International executives manage their enterprises on shifting foundations. Often they are not quite aware of how or why conditions are changing until they find themselves in trouble. This is not meant to suggest that overseas managers deliberately practice managerial brinkmanship, even though it might be convenient for them to do so when direction from top management is not clearly defined. Quite the contrary, international executives have to contend with problems resulting from too many unknowns and too little information; they are confronted with a wide range of alternatives, and many of them lack the accumulated experience necessary to resolve their difficulties.

Even men who have been exposed to both sides of the international fence sometimes

---

* From a paper presented by Dr. Wertheimer before the convention of the Association for Education in International Business at the New York Hilton Hotel, December 29, 1965.

fall into a trap. A French executive who worked on both sides—as a regional manager based at headquarters and as a general manager of an overseas subsidiary—attributed many of his headaches in the two jobs to the unreliability of data. In his opinion, the major challenges in both assignments were (1) achieving communications reliability, (2) semantics, and (3) the use of mechanical media for data transmission. He said:

> In international industrial operations, as in domestic operations, we base decisions on the information we receive. But, unlike domestic operations, we can depend much less on this information because it does not meet the minimum standard required for able decision making. Reliability, then, becomes the number one challenge.

Whether they like it or not, headquarters executives are often stuck with what the subsidiaries send them, and the subsidiaries, with what they receive from headquarters. Between his two international assignments, the French executive cited above was in charge of programming support at headquarters and instituted a policy of software acceptance on a total-systems basis. The policy was to be applicable to all domestic and international operations except those that were "far away." This exception was based strictly on "budgetary reasoning."

Later the executive was appointed general manager of a distant subsidiary that had been excluded from the software-acceptance test. Because of the policy he had introduced, his operations had software bugs, local implementation difficulties, and subsequent loss of revenue. Ironically, when he addressed himself to headquarters as a subsidiary general manager with the request that the situation be remedied, the reply came back that, since he himself had established the policy, he had better live with it.

It is indeed difficult for the men at headquarters to think about the subsidiary's problems while they are carrying out their daily activities. And it is equally difficult for the men at the subsidiary to put themselves in the shoes of the men at headquarters. No wonder communication crises develop when requests remain unanswered because responsible executives minimize their urgency, consider them low-priority, or disregard them. Nor does the manager on the other side think in the same terms and act in the same way as headquarters men who make the requests.

Filtering requests, and classifying them on a rational basis, requires extensive knowledge about a company, its subsidiaries, and the countries in which they operate, as well as familiarity with the problems at hand. Few executives fully meet these qualifications. And those who are qualified still have to combat numerous problems, including the risk that a unique channel will turn into a screen, dividing rather than uniting the two ends.

Blocked or crowded channels invariably cause managers to escape their responsibilities by a series of machinations that range from simple buck passing to formal resignation. It should not come as a surprise that many overseas executives wonder if there is a better way to earn a living. What seems remarkable is that such a large number of them are willing to continue in jobs that are so frustrating.

Within his lifetime the professional manager assigned abroad is exposed to conflicting management philosophies and incompatible methodologies. He finds it difficult to unlearn many of the principles presented at school and practiced in the early years of his career. Conventional management education programs have done little to illuminate the differences between country-of-origin and multinational operations.

Faced with conflicts of interest, changes,

and unfamiliar situations, the international manager builds bulwarks to guard against the invasion of his management domain. At best he finds it difficult to remain vigorous and creative and to continue pioneering. But even the international manager who remains creative and active, and does all sorts of courageous things, needs to keep two-way channels open to insure that his drive does not come to a standstill.

Attitudes and Feelings

A point made by several international executives was that communication problems often get worse before they get better. Said the general manager of a foreign subsidiary: "It gives one a helpless feeling when every year things seem worse than in the preceding year." The manager's concern is very real.

Even foreign executives who said there was nothing wrong with their companies' communications systems admitted that the systems were not prompt and effective and that improvements were needed. Their comments usually referred to the day-to-day demands of the job; the executives seldom discussed the practical necessities of dealing with public and social responsibilities, which are especially important in diverse or unfavorable environments. Meeting such responsibilities places an additional demand on the physical and operational aspects of communication.

One factor that adds considerable strain to the communications network of a multinational company is mistrust. It is both irksome and irrational. Headquarters sometimes looks upon general managers of foreign subsidiaries—whether they are country-of-origin nationals, local nationals, or third-country men—exactly as a bank clerk would regard a customer carrying a re-

volver. Cameron McKenzie identified this condition as follows:

> Foreign operations that complain of incompetent general managers usually have at least three things in common. First, they have overextensive control systems; that is, headquarters demands data that are useless for evaluating performance and for communicating its objectives to the local management or motivating it to reach them. Second, the manager really has no grasp of what is going on, even though his reports may be current and correct. A third common symptom is the irrational fashion in which the manager reacts to either verbal or written instructions. If such symptoms exist, management will be well advised to take a careful look at its control system before passing judgment on its manager.*

Under these conditions the executive on assignment abroad cannot develop. His progress is curtailed by repetitive controls on minimatters and low ceilings imposed by overextensive controls. His wings are clipped further when headquarters complains about trivialities. Less evident, but equally dangerous, is the effect on morale and the development of human potential caused by overcrowding of the communications network. In the same article, Cameron McKenzie described the situation:

> Ultimately the foreign general manager loses (or never develops) the sense of responsibility and proprietary interest that is essential for a chief operating executive to have. He becomes a man on a string, being pulled this way and that by headquarters demands, attempting to satisfy not the needs of the business but of his advisors. He is no longer managing a system on whose smooth and successful operation profit depends, but a series of disconnected functions.

---

* *Cameron McKenzie, "Incompetent Foreign Managers?" Business Horizons,* Spring 1966.

Thus one ingredient is essential for sound communication in international organizations: managerial confidence. This was confirmed and illustrated during interviews with numerous international executives. They squarely placed the emphasis on obtained results, rather than pieces of paper. These international executives stated that work schedules built around goals—instead of crowded conventional reporting—would enable them to make a greater contribution in fewer hours. But work habits are so firmly established that companies would undoubtedly have to induce their executives to become more productive and stop battling paper tigers.

Participating executives were concerned with issues such as whether "new communications technologies are made available to the subsidiary fast enough" and whether "the subsidiary is getting the full benefit of the improvements in communications media." But knowledgeable executives, at headquarters and abroad, recognized that there are more important issues, one of which is the development and utilization of manpower and other resources.

Of course, paperwork does serve some real needs: It provides vital data; it informs; and it builds fences. But what executives sometimes forget is that paperwork is not an end in itself and that the information reported is only a surface representation of reality.

An example was provided by an administrator in sub-Saharan Africa in a personal letter he wrote to a university professor:

> There are more educated idiots with Ph.D.'s wandering around Africa than any other area in the world. None of them knows a thing about business and they are trying out all kinds of weird theories on these poor people. They talk to them about micro- and macro-economics and cost accounting theories and productivity.... Meanwhile, it takes one ton of paper and two years' time to process a small loan....

It might be more precise to talk of two tons of paper: one required by the local government and the other by the company's own headquarters. In most of the operating subsidiaries visited in Mexico, Guatemala, San Salvador, Nicaragua, Panama, and Venezuela, and in countries of Western Europe, overreporting was prevalent. Said the general manager of an American subsidiary in Panama:

> The reporting structure is just too heavy. We are two country-of-origin executives here, the treasurer and myself. He checks on the treasury and I watch profit-and-loss and sales figures. Each one of us is snowed under tons of paper. We have to watch not only the quantity but also the quality.
>
> The report to the chief executive officer is an example of what I mean. In preparing it I have to watch every "if" and "but"; so it takes the better part of a day. This is also the most productive part of the day, since it has to be the time when I am fully alert. One cannot approach such a report with a confused, tired, or hazy mind.

What can executives overdepending on heavy communications loads expect to achieve? The greater the flow of information, the less significant each report seems and the more burdensome the reporting process becomes. It is unlikely that subsidiary executives will ever agree with the leather-eared skeptics who maintain that we will learn to live with the paper jungle or that the executives will ever tolerate experts who imply that unless performance is analyzed it is of little value to the company.

In one major corporation, the chief executive suspected that information was being duplicated; so he asked all persons at headquarters and in the subsidiaries to carefully evaluate the various reports traveling back and forth. This example provides a significant point: Unless the top man in the organization takes things into his own hands by assuming an active role in communication, there is almost no hope of stopping the flood of unnecessary reports, letters, cables, and calls.

The general impression among many headquarters people is that they must write often to foreign executives who are thousands of miles away. Not only is the value of such correspondence unestablished; but, in addition, overcrowded communications networks waste much valuable time and cost more than they are worth. Therefore, top men at home and abroad need to keep an eye on the situation so that the systems do not drift off course.

Conditions for Effecting Changes

In international business, the most effective executive decision making is a systematic process with clearly defined elements, each of which requires appropriate information. Other aspects of the international management process also have to be analyzed and defined so that specifications can be made, information needs established, and boundaries drawn. To perform these activities, the executive must communicate. No matter how skilled and how knowledgeable he may be, he cannot gain the acceptance for, or achieve, the compromises, adaptations, and concessions necessary to do his job if he does not communicate. Nor can he obtain feedback to find out how effective his decisions are and how well they are being implemented by others.

While some international executives stated that their companies' present communications systems were inadequate, others were not so direct in their reaction. But the expressions on their faces told a lot. Responsible executives emphasized that frequently information is handled inefficiently either because the executives are inexperienced or because there is too much resistance to overcome. Which is to say that experience in communication, and the desire for better communication, are lacking.

Much depends on which is more important to corporate management: bureaucratic reporting or an information system with some semblance of order and efficiency. No company can have it both ways. Some have tried, but the result is usually that they have it neither way.

Most senior executives in multinational firms know that communications often are verbose or incomplete or have "soft spots" in their interpretation. These flaws are not attributable to language, even though linguistic problems make matters worse. Nor can they be overcome by verbal skills or personal magnetism. There is a wide range of environmental differences and individual differences, such as background and experience, and the personal characteristics considered desirable in one country may be unacceptable in another.

Companies that have entered the international industrial scene frequently bring from their domestic operations one especially bad habit: putting more emphasis on the methods used to communicate information than on the kind of information transmitted. For example, speed has become an obsession, often at the expense of accuracy. This increases the need for a precise definition of what a company wants, needs, and can afford to pump into its communications network.

Justice Oliver Wendell Holmes once said, "The life of the law is not logic, but experience." This maxim also applies to business. Companies operating in varied environments should not be overly dependent on logic in seeking solutions to their communication problems. They need to be more eager to test the waters, evaluate results, knock down unnecessary fences, and insure greater participation.

The role of headquarters in an industrial empire is not to impose parental discipline on fractious subsidiaries and affiliates, but to encourage viable relationships brought about by common self-interest. This approach calls for analyzing the principles that make relationships viable and for articulating and extending them to gain general acceptance. This approach also breaks up companies' anachronistic practices, which this study found to be the cause of many problems and limitations in communication.

In most industrial organizations, it must be added, when certain relationships become unviable the principles underlying them vanish. Then executives eager to make a contribution waste no time mourning, but focus their attention on the active relationships that remain and the new ones that emerge. But, in international business, principles and policies respond more slowly to changing relationships and conditions because of the distance between the executives who set the policies and those on the operating levels.

Clearcut specifications about what the company needs to accomplish are essential in establishing sound communication practices. So are brevity and the realistic establishment of priorities. Because communication priorities are so difficult to establish, especially in international business, a few corporations follow the "Eisenhower rule." One of President Eisenhower's assistants told the author that, when the President took office, he asked his immediate assistants and Cabinet members to submit reports that were brief, factual, and documented. The President was reported to have made this statement:

If you give me a half-page report I promise to read it right away. If you submit a one-

page report I will read it sometime today but not immediately. If you give me a two-page report I will still read it, but I cannot say when. If the report is longer than two typewritten pages I will not read it.

The story goes that Cabinet members and assistants kept pouring heavy reports onto the President's desk. To show them that he meant what he had said, President Eisenhower tore off the first two pages of each report and kept them in his file for subsequent reading. The other pages he threw into the wastebasket. This type of response is far more effective than a strongly worded memorandum, but few executives are able to take such measures.

The magnitude of prevailing international communication problems correctly reflects the transition that management itself is undergoing. Most executives know that currently available information systems do not satisfy companies' basic communications needs. Many systems are ineffectual and inappropriate, and may be worse than an earlier type of communications network that was structurally out of balance but did a good job at the time.

International management has just begun to realize that inoperative communications channels can and should be closed down at the first opportunity. The impulse for doing so is strong because appropriate elements from today's communications jungle can be salvaged, while keeping a system intact tends to multiply existing problems. Clear thinking is needed to determine if and when specific reports or channels should be abandoned and to insure that executives are not overly complacent about existing methods.

Quite frequently, because companies fail to clarify factors that cause existing problems, situations are left unsolved, with the hope that some point-by-point settlements will evolve. Interviews confirmed that some companies have studied their communication problems and have seriously considered alternatives—even though the first round of correspondence and discussions with most executives at company headquarters resulted in comments such as: "We are so well organized that we face no communication problems."

Since few companies are totally married to their current communication schemes, one can assume that their failure to make changes stems partially from simple resistance or inertia. Also, many managers seem to believe that the real challenges to communication will continue to come from within rather than from without the company. Every day, additional burdens are added to existing information networks. Expansion and diversification of companies have increased the number of environments to which systems must respond. The number of countries in which the companies operate has increased, and rapidly developing technologies create new vulnerabilities for many communications networks, as do ever changing international political and economic factors.

The fact that the headquarters of multinational companies are not altogether unaware of the prevailing situation, and the risks that it can bring, is encouraging. Until recently, headquarters' limited understanding about its communications with foreign subsidiaries seemed to be leading them to Utopian ideas of what is possible. Since communication is one of the least standardized activities in the entire management spectrum, idealistic solutions are inappropriate.

But anyone ready to give three cheers to the spirit of change in communication will have to think again. Change will come slowly—too slowly by many standards. While some myths lie dead in the ashes of miscommunication, many problems remain. No two companies have followed the same formula in gearing communications to international operations. Wide gaps exist in the working relationships between companies' international units and the domestic operating groups. In many companies management cannot even keep up with past and present problems, let alone think about future ones.

2. Communication Practices Illustrated

Conducting research on international communication problems at the operational level enables one to see that actual needs and interests can diverge considerably from theories and assumptions. The closer one gets to companies' ongoing activities, the more apparent this becomes. Although attention was focused on the mechanics and dynamics of communication at all levels, it was the subsidiaries that sounded the alarm regarding the magnitude of difficulty that they and others are experiencing.

When asked how the dynamics of communication affect his company, Dr. William F. Ballhaus, president of Beckman Instruments Inc., provided the following summary:

> Primarily, the structure of communications internal to the company is tailored to satisfy the customers' requirements. Secondary considerations are the configuration of the organization, geographic disbursement of facilities, complexity of information to be communicated, frequency of types of communications, and timeliness of data. Fast, straightforward transmission and short lines of communication are used for handling any information directly with the customer. Highly technical material is transmitted so that the recipient is in direct contact with the generating body. The communication of general management information in the majority of instances conforms to patterns dictated by the organizational and responsibility assignments in the corporation.

Ten specific questions were asked of key participants in this study. Emphasis was placed on the types of communications channels within the companies and the way these channels work, with the hope that overall approaches and attitudes would be unveiled. The questions were as follows:

1. Who communicates with whom in headquarters and in the subsidiary?
2. What are the subjects of these communications?
3. What methods of communication are used?
4. How often do communications occur?
5. What factors are taken into account regarding reliability and interpretation of communications?
6. How are priorities determined?
7. Are agenda prepared for meetings? What are the topics?
8. How often are subsidiary executives asked to come to headquarters and vice versa?
9. To what extent are communications coordinated? By what means?
10. What are considered the main causes of communication barriers? To what extent do international companies think through and carry out actions to overcome these barriers?

The most succinct response to these questions was provided by one international executive: "Like banana skins, solutions to communications problems can in some contexts be protective, in others catastrophic." Another executive, who had worldwide experience, said that in redesigning a multinational communications system companies would do well to follow the advice given by George Moore when he was chief executive officer of First National City Bank of New York: "Be brave enough to scare Chase, but never be brave enough to scare me." This type of stand is often necessary to close the gap between expectations and outcomes.

The following sections of this chapter contain some of the best written replies to the author's inquiries. In these responses, executives discuss financial and technical burdens, as well as other obstacles that companies encounter in the communication process. Less is said about revamping channels; but, as the author has stated so often, this need is one of the most urgent problems in industry today.

Persons Who Communicate

Beckman Instruments Inc. is a multi-division company that manufactures a variety of highly technical products. Each of its eight major domestic divisions specializes in a group of products that are marketed in the fields of medicine, industry, education, and scientific research. Internationally, the organizations and manufacturing facilities are geographically oriented and tend to serve specific areas, such as the European Economic Community, the European Free Trade Association, and Latin America. The total company is, therefore, geographically as well as market-oriented.

Beckman Instruments has a high volume of international communications among its various international, corporate, and domestic division marketing personnel. Foreign sales subsidiaries, franchised dealers, and customers deal directly with domestic manufacturing divisions regarding the supply of products. International headquarters and export department personnel situated at or near division facilities serve as an interface between foreign and domestic communicants. In effect, the domestic divisions' technical specialists handle all subjects related to the technical aspects of products, while the international subsidiaries' trade specialists communicate about the customs, commercial, and traffic aspects of the transactions. A corporate marketing services department coordinates communications between domestic and foreign marketing groups about advertising, sales brochures, and other sales promotion materials.

Communications relating to the management of international operations are handled on a typical line-staff basis. The director of foreign operations, situated at corporate headquarters, reports directly to the president. The vice presidents of finance, manufacturing, marketing, and personnel; the directors of research, engineering, and product planning; and the controller, the treasurer, and the legal counsel perform staff functions for the president involving communications with foreign manufacturing and sales subsidiary personnel. Domestic manufacturing division personnel give foreign subsidiaries direct support on specific projects.

Hughes Aircraft Company has a number of communications channels between several levels of headquarters and the foreign affiliates; these channels vary according to subject matter. There is a constant flow of technical communications between the engineers and the technicians to insure that the affiliates and licensees are supported in their programs and, in turn, to insure that the company benefits from any technical advances resulting from the operations. On the corporate side, these communications are conducted by technical people in the operating divisions that have product responsibility for the programs.

The company has an international group and, within it, a joint venture and license administration department that represents the Hughes interests in the day-to-day operations of these affiliates and provides coordination among them. Communications between members of this department and the affiliates' operating executives relate mostly to marketing and financial matters and to the administration of agreements between the company and affiliates. All communications regarding policies or major decisions are conducted between the international group executive and the top executives of the affiliates.

In the Singer Company, communication between corporate headquarters and the field exists at all levels and in all directions —that is, corporate staff to the field, field to corporate staff, field to division headquarters, division headquarters to field, and so forth. Under normal conditions, most corporate staff communications, or division communications, are funneled through the general manager of the field organizational group.

Honeywell Inc. has an international division consisting of five regions: the United Kingdom–Scandinavia, Continental Europe, South America, the Far East, and Canada. The subsidiary personnel within a region communicate with people in the regional headquarters and the U.S. parent company and directly with one another when necessary. Usually, divisional personnel communicate with other people in their product line. Each of the company's ten divisions has an international marketing manager at the division's U.S. headquarters. (Headquarters are situated in several U.S. cities.)

The five regions are managed by vice presidents, much of whose communication is with the corporate vice president in charge of the international division. Subsidiary managers, in turn, communicate with their regional vice presidents and keep them informed about communications with divisional people in the United States.

Aerojet-General Corporation has an in-

ternational operations division at corporate headquarters in El Monte, California. Copies of all important correspondence are sent to this office, which permits coordination by a central group and eliminates duplication of effort in the various divisions. Although international employees of the various plants communicate directly with employees in corporate's international operations, they send copies to the division.

An important source of information is Aerojet's office in Washington, D.C., in which representatives keep posted on Government rules and regulations regarding overseas trade.

A major tire manufacturer has more traditional channels of communication. There are three international regions—Europe, Asia-Africa, and the Western Hemisphere—headed by directors whose offices are situated in the headquarters of the international corporation. The managing directors of the subsidiary companies report to and communicate with the three regional directors; the sales directors in the field report to and communicate primarily with the regional sales vice presidents; the production directors report to the production managers at headquarters; the finance people report to the financial vice president and controller; and so forth.

At Libbey-Owens-Ford Company, communications of overseas subsidiaries are directed to the export department. Who writes to whom is determined by the subject. If it is a policy matter, or something financial, it is usually handled by the president of the subsidiary and the president of the export company. If it conveys orders or technical information, the man at the subsidiary would correspond with the general manager of the export company.

Carnation Company has one division that is concerned with management of and relations with the company's foreign subsidiaries. Situated in Los Angeles, the division has its own president and other officers. Subsidiary executives are free to communicate with any employee of the parent company and its product divisions. However, most communications occur on the divisional level—that is, the financial executive of the foreign subsidiary communicates with the financial executive of the U.S. division, the subsidiary sales executive with the sales executive of the U.S. division, and so forth.

At Olivetti Corporation the specific persons or departments to communicate with a subsidiary are determined by the nature of the communication; namely:

1. Matters involving major policy problems and decisions, depending on the nature of the subject:
   • The president, for all communications concerning group structure.
   • The managing directors, for matters of special interest involving a top management decision.
   • The general sales manager.
2. Matters involving specialized subjects, when specific knowledge of problems is required:
   • The director of marketing, acting in his staff relationship to the general sales manager.
   • In certain cases, specialists (product managers) of the marketing divisions.
3. Routine matters, which are referred to other departments, such as finance and administration.

Communications are generally addressed to the managing director of the subsidiary, except in the highly diversified subsidiaries that have levels corresponding with each of the levels mentioned above. In such cases, many communications are lateral.

In one company that preferred remaining anonymous—which will be called Company A—the participating executive commented that each function usually communicates with its counterpart function at other locations. The company's top management recognizes that communication is one of the biggest problems in business today and encourages the functional executives to write directly to the location where they think they can obtain an answer. When the executives communicate directly, management requests that they inform the appropriate individuals by sending copies along the chain of command. When a person does not know whom to write for information and needs assistance to obtain an answer, he also goes through the chain of command in the headquarters of a country or an area.

In another unidentified company—Company B—an international marketing group was organized and was supposed to receive all international communications. According to a senior executive of the company, this group lacks competence in so many areas that it is often short-circuited by subsidiary personnel, who want direct answers from knowledgeable people. Those communications that are sent to the group have to be routed to others; so the group's office is little more than a mailroom.

People in the subsidiary often call or write to headquarters people whom they know personally—regardless of their positions—to request information, get help on particular prospects, and obtain other types of assistance. This practice is prevalent among subsidiary people who are Americans, especially if they formerly worked in the home office.

Very often the subsidiary feels it will not get sufficient attention at headquarters if it uses the usual channels. Therefore, an "ambassador" is selected to represent the subsidiary at headquarters and to follow up on its problems. Sometimes this job is used for management training, in which case people are rotated once a year.

Subjects Communicated

In response to the author's query about subject matter, Millard H. Pryor, Jr., director of product policy of the Singer Company (now vice president, Industrial Products Division), commented briefly: "Communications involve every subject normally discussed in a business environment."

Dr. William F. Ballhaus divides topics of communication into four categories: technical, marketing, manufacturing, and general management. Technical subjects are included in research and development reports, product evaluation studies, product planning reports, research coordination information, directives related to design criteria, component standardization procedures and instructions, and research personnel utilization reports.

Marketing communications involving direct contact with customers relate to product specifications, prices, delivery, repair and installation service, clarification about commercial orders, expediting, shipment instructions, and methods and terms of payment. Within the marketing department, topics of information transfer include sales policies, market evaluation information, forecasts and quotas, new-product ideas, selling and servicing aids, sales call reports, product specifications and pricing details, advertising, product effectiveness, quality of product and service, exhibition and sales promotion projects, dealer and customer training materials, sales-volume reports, selling-expense reports, inventory levels, customer service reports, distribution assignments, personnel utilization, and general marketing management communications.

Manufacturing requires coordination between product-oriented domestic divisions and geographically oriented foreign organizations and therefore involves communications about product specifications, manufacturing drawings, production techniques, tooling requirements, assembly-cost studies, purchasing information, product standardization policies, quality control practices, production personnel training, make-or-buy decisions, selection of products, factory loading, industrial engineering practices, and general manufacturing management policies.

General management topics in international communications span all corporate activities, which include finance, taxation, patents and copyrights, distribution channels, and personnel, in addition to research, marketing, and plant supervision.

R. L. Michelson, manager of customer relations of Honeywell's international division, said that in general his company's international communications relate to finance, personnel, delivery, pricing, facilities (offices, warehouses, and factories), bidding on jobs, sales promotion, advertising, public relations, exchange of visits (both company people and customers), development of new devices, marketing, training, competition, establishment of distributors (in areas where Honeywell is not already represented), and coordination of jobs when more than one subsidiary is involved.

The senior executive of the participating tire company commented that three types of subjects might be discussed between operating groups in the field and the staff at headquarters: policy matters, operating opportunities, and problems.

The executive in Company A provided this summary:

All types of subjects are involved, but the usual ones are those relating to operations of the business—specifically, company policies, letters of instruction, educational programs, budget matters, and manpower staffing problems.

In contrast, the executive in Company B classified subjects into two general types:

The usual "official" subjects are information on orders, shipments, customer visits, and so forth. "Unofficial" subjects are requests for technical information, appeals for help, and grapevine communications on organizational changes.

Methods Used

Three main modes of communication were reported: mail (correspondence and fairly lengthy reports); rapid transmissions (telephone, intercom connections, teletype, and telegrams); and face-to-face meetings (at headquarters, subsidiary offices, and elsewhere). The relative importance of these methods varies substantially with the company, the product, and the geographic area, as well as with the novelty of the task.

Dr. Ballhaus analyzed the methods used at Beckman Instruments:

About 60 percent of all international communications are written communications in the form of letters, memoranda, and printed materials. Most of this volume is dispatched by airmail, with an occasional large shipment of heavy materials by air printed matter or commercial freight.

A second category of written communications, composing about 20 percent of the total, consists of cables, TWX's (teletypes), and telexes. Oral communications represent the balance of 20 percent, and can be split about equally between telephone and direct contact. Recent trends are to utilize more direct oral communications and leased-line telex service and to reduce considerably the written mail communications.

Dr. Ballhaus' remarks stimulated the author to make a statistical evaluation of the methods used in a variety of companies and under different operating environments. The quantitative results of this research are presented in Chapter 3, together with relevant commentaries. A summary of the methods used by nine participating companies follows:

- At Hughes International Inc., the day-to-day communications are generally written and transmitted by mail or teletype, depending upon their urgency. It is common practice for technical personnel to be exchanged; that is, transferred from one area to another, to insure a clear flow of data. Furthermore, the Hughes Aircraft International Service Company operates foreign offices in Europe and the Far East, and the personnel of these offices maintain contact with the affiliates in their areas.
- Singer, in addition to communicating by letter, uses a telex connection between the United States and Europe, cablegrams, and, increasingly, the long-distance telephone.
- Honeywell communicates primarily by memoranda (letters), but also uses telephone and telex extensively. The company has leased wire facilities between the United States and Europe for rapid communication, when it is necessary.

- Aerojet-General's policies call for written communications to be used consistently and for telephone calls to be kept to a minimum.
- At Libbey-Owens-Ford, communication is primarily by letter. However, corporate management stresses the necessity of frequent visits by personnel who are concerned with the activities of subsidiary companies. Said one company executive: "This is about the only way that complete meetings of the mind can be assured."
- Olivetti has no established methods or special procedures. The only important factor is achieving desired results.
- Company A follows this practice: telephone when an immediate answer is required, telex for a 24-hour answer, and letter for the normal communication cycle.
- Company B indicated that communication by letter is used less than other methods because (1) it takes too long and (2) most people are too busy to answer letters. The use of telex is the most frequent, since one can usually get a reply the following day. Communication by telephone is also frequent, despite the cost, for very urgent or complex matters and for matters that need to be negotiated—and to reach persons who do not answer letters or telexes.
- Company C—another firm that requested anonymity—uses these methods: letters, oral communication through face-to-face meetings in the United States and abroad, and seminars, symposiums, and conventions for sales representatives, scientists, systems specialists, customer service people, and others. This company also has a private wire network linking most of its facilities and used extensively.

Frequency of Communication

One executive commented that literally hundreds of international messages are passed daily through the various transmission media of his company. In addition, at any given time an average of three to four persons are traveling to accomplish direct, oral communication. In another company, a typical large subsidiary receives from ten to twenty pieces of correspondence a day, while a smaller subsidiary may receive from five to ten such communications a day.

According to one executive, his company believes that minimum levels of communication should be established to insure that channels are kept open and that relationships can be maintained. Beyond this, the frequency of communication depends upon the level of activity. In still another company, communications are constant: Cables, telephone calls, and letters are exchanged at headquarters in volume.

Obviously, frequency of communication is a factor that could use some sort of standardization and some criteria to improve efficiency. But knowledgeable executives would be the first to admit that frequency of communication cannot be standardized until many unnecessary nuts and bolts are removed. And international companies are still a long way from that point.

Said an executive of a leading electronics corporation:

Frequency of communications has no specific pattern in our business. The usual statistical report is required monthly, quarterly, and annually. General types of communications vary, depending on changes in company products, policies, and procedures. Special projects develop requirements that differ from daily, weekly, and monthly communications, and even from those made on a demand basis.

A second company reported "no set standard," and a third, that its communications are "as frequent as circumstances call for."

In the opinion of Elserino Piol, of Olivetti, communication frequencies of a subsidiary vary with its size and importance, and the particular moment of its life. According to Pier A. Abetti, an international executive of European background, now with General Electric Company in Phoenix, Arizona, variation is also a matter of corporate policy:

When I was with Univac, I made an average of one telephone call to the United States every working day, and I sent four or five telexes, but only one letter. With Bull General Electric, I made fewer phone calls, but sent more telexes.

Of course, frequency of communication can be standardized for some types of information. Monthly reports are an example, as one company indicated: "Monthly reports are received on predetermined, fixed dates, but other communications are exchanged freely as the occasions arise." Aerojet-General's corporate headquarters "receives a written monthly report from the Paris office and one from the Orion-Aerojet office in Germany. Letters on various subjects are transmitted as required."

When one examines matters outside the reporting framework, companies tend to be a bit vaguer about the frequency of their communication. They mention general criteria such as (1) necessity and (2) needs based on experience. One multinational combine characterized frequency as "constant." Said the participating executive:

With more than 16,000 employees overseas, and a direct wire to Europe, communications are so easy that they become almost burdensome. Our mail load is enormous. As a matter of fact, we are taking steps to cut down in order to save money. We use a bulletin system to announce certain kinds of information that is of interest to everyone, such as price changes, address changes, personnel appointments, and model changes. We have different mailing lists for the different types of bulletins, and these are constantly reviewed to keep them current and to eliminate unnecessary distribution.

In some international firms, top management is aware that communications rates and frequencies need to undergo a careful filtering. A headquarters executive said that in his company "communication occurs on a weekly basis, and in many instances on a daily basis, to take up the various problems." But other headquarters executives and most executives abroad believe that high frequency is becoming too cumbersome.

An important consideration is the quality of the communication. Quickly assembled statistics and speedily written reports have enough cracks to seriously hamper decision making at headquarters. Area executives who have to build on these reports want them to be accurate and complete. Subsidiary managers, in turn, need quality and find that watching for it is most time consuming. Quality is particularly important in reports to the president and vice presidents, in financial statements, control data, and many other reports.

A subsidiary general manager in Central America described his experience:

Last February I kept records on how I was spending my time. Somehow, I could not figure how the days went by so fast. I included every single thing that I did during the day, even my visits to the men's room.

Time is tricky. I knew that I was doing my best and was working with reasonable efficiency; still, I was meeting no more than two key customers per week. The rest of the week was taken with communications and with matters that only I could do, such as writing proposals to the Government. As my study showed, the most time-consuming item was the reports. Never before had I realized the great delays involved in collecting one's own data and in choosing one's own words—every single one of them.

Determinants of Reliability

At Beckman Instruments, the communications channel between the factory and the customers abroad generally involves language translation. The majority of these translations are done by the foreign subsidiaries or franchised dealers in their day-to-day activities. The company's international headquarters and export department maintain a staff of language specialists to assist with written correspondence with customers when the need arises. All international field sales and service specialists are bilingual or multilingual. Sales literature or other printed materials intended for direct distribution to customers are printed in all major languages.

Considerable attention is given to the form and structure of all communications. Concise, brief but detailed messages are stressed. Emphasis is placed on trying to put oneself "in the position of the recipient" and communicating clearly. Thus the company declares: "If the communication can be misunderstood, it will be!"

The risk of misinterpretation is indeed great, and quite well recognized by a rather large number of the companies participating in this study. This points up the need for filtering—and the risks involved in the process. One participant said: "When receiving communications from individuals, we usually take into consideration their degree of familiarity with English and their known moods and outlooks." Another one said that in his firm "each area has its own factors and means of determining the effectiveness of its communications."

Company A described its communication procedures:

Before a numerically controlled letter is mailed out, an authorization sheet is sent with a draft of the letter to the appropriate functions so they can verify the content. This procedure helps to provide the correct facts in a manner that is easy for the countries to understand. Also, it keeps the company from overlooking functions that should have a voice in a particular subject.

For other types of letters, not under numerical control, copies are usually directed to individuals who may have a need to know, are experienced in a specific subject or location, and are asked to comment about correctness.

Other reactions concerning the reliability of communications were positive; for example:

• Reliability and interpretation of communications pose no problems. This company has been engaged in international business for half a century. We feel we know fairly well how to communicate across oceans and national boundaries.
• We have no difficulty regarding reliability or interpretation of communications.
• Our experience thus far has not given us any reason to doubt the reliability or interpretation of communications from our foreign affiliates.

Setting Priorities

According to Dr. Ballhaus, customer service problems have top priority at Beckman Instruments. Specific policies have been established for communication, order handling, and other activities to reflect the emphasis on rapid service for customers. Priorities are designated on communiqués by using the terms "urgent" or "immediate." The company follows the standard practice of answering a cable with a cable, a telephone call with a telephone call, and so forth.

Aerojet's policy calls for priorities to be determined on the basis of what a particular division can offer a foreign country or company and the volume of business that will be realized from a contact. Other companies determine priorities by the urgency of the situation. For instance, a cable or telephone message asking for immediate response will receive priority over a routine letter. This was the underlying spirit of many answers:

- Priorities in communication are determined by the general business criteria of importance and urgency.
- Our communications priorities are determined by the relative importance of each communication.
- Communications priorities are based on expected results and the effect on the company as a whole.
- Priorities are determined by keeping in mind the interests of the group as a whole.
- Priorities are established by experience . . . usually on an emergency basis.

Company D's priorities are determined on the basis of the individual situation: "There is no formal pattern to follow in our company. We have established due dates for certain reports, which, of course, take precedence over general types of communications." An executive at Company E said:

We do not establish any particular priorities with regard to who communicates with whom—or how. Occasionally there is some determination as to whether an item should be discussed over the phone or dealt with

by cable, telex, or letter. This is entirely subjective, and is dealt with by the individual in charge.

Preparation of Agenda

Although responses to this question varied, the overwhelming majority of the participating companies were in favor of formal agenda. At Beckman Instruments, most itineraries and agenda are carefully coordinated prior to meetings or foreign travel. The topics differ according to the line or staff positions of the persons involved and the specific problems considered important at the time.

Hughes International follows a similar practice. Agenda are generally prepared for these visits by the executive of the host company who is responsible for coordinating and administering the affiliate. In addition to having the many managerial capabilities required for these positions, the executives of the joint venture and license administration department—which administers and coordinates affiliate activities—have to be conversant in the language of the affiliate.

Agenda as such are not usually prepared at Honeywell, unless several regional and/or subsidiary managers get together and a formal meeting is conducted. This happens infrequently, explained R. L. Michelson, manager of customer relations of the international division. Review meetings are held twice a year, when the regional managers tell top management what they have accomplished and what they expect to accomplish in the future. Budgets are usually prepared late in the fall and reviewed about midyear.

At Singer Company, said Millard H. Pryor, "Agenda are usually prepared if there is a specific purpose for the meeting." Practices cited by executives in other participating companies are as follows:

• Agenda are prepared for the yearly meeting. Topics vary according to the immediate need for information. (Aerojet-General)

• Agenda are usually prepared for meetings between headquarters and subsidiary executives, and are based on current topics. (Libbey-Owens-Ford)

• In all cases agenda are prepared for meetings at headquarters. These agenda are very formal for the annual meetings and less formal, but nonetheless specific, for other meetings. (Procter and Gamble)

• Informal agenda are prepared for meetings relating to general management problems. (American Standard)

• Agenda for meetings are prepared by both the subsidiary and the headquarters, although not necessarily on a uniform basis. (Olivetti)

• Specific functional meetings have agenda. All the other types of visits are handled on a less formal basis. Subjects discussed relate to local situations, demands of the business, and new policies or products to be announced. (Company A)

• Agenda are prepared for formal meetings once or twice a year, at which time business is reviewed and planning sessions are conducted. These agenda are usually very concise. (Company B)

• Agenda are prepared for some meetings, but other meetings are informal. The topics cover every business aspect of the foreign subsidiary's operation. (Company C)

• Agenda are prepared for headquarters–subsidiary meetings; in general, the topics cover sales, production, development, personnel, advertising, public relations, and so on. (Company D)

Visits of Executives

Here reactions vary considerably, not only between companies but also within the same company. For example, Beckman In-struments' eight foreign subsidiaries differ considerably in size, functional purpose, and organizational structure. Two wholly owned subsidiaries have manufacturing and marketing responsibilities. One company is a joint venture. The other subsidiaries have several forms of marketing and sales organizations. Thus the frequency of executive visits varies for a number of reasons.

"Generally speaking," said Dr. Ballhaus, "the larger and more complex the subsidiary operation, the more frequently its executives visit headquarters and the more frequently they are visited by headquarters personnel." An average of four to five executives from each of the two largest (manufacturing) subsidiaries visit headquarters once or twice a year for an average visit of three weeks. Visits by corporate personnel occur as often, but the duration of their visits averages only about one week. Executives of the three medium-size subsidiaries average three visits to headquarters per year, one by each key executive. The subsidiaries, in turn, are visited every year by approximately three executives from the parent company. The smaller overseas organizations are geographically widespread sales companies. Although they have a large number of direct contacts with sales specialists, they average only one visit a year by a corporate executive. Managers of these sales companies visit headquarters about once a year.

R. W. Lindgren, manager of administration, said that at Hughes International executives from wholly owned subsidiaries usually visit the California headquarters twice a year. Headquarters executives visit each foreign location at least once a year, usually in conjunction with the annual board meeting. The same frequency generally prevails for joint ventures, although this depends more on the level of business activity. These visits do not include the exchange of technical personnel.

Singer's policy states that subsidiary executives are to visit New York once a year, but two trips every other year probably is more typical. Honeywell has no formal pattern. Visits to some subsidiaries are more frequent than to others. Regional vice presidents visit headquarters more frequently than the subsidiary managers do. And headquarters people visit the subsidiaries more often than the subsidiary people visit the United States.

An international company that has licensing agreements with European firms—rather than subsidiaries—establishes different communication patterns. W. E. Burdwick, manager, international operations, Aerojet-General Corporation, described his company's patterns:

> Aerojet-General has a slightly different approach to its international communications in that we do a majority of our work through licensing and technical agreements with other countries. We have no overseas subsidiaries as such, but do maintain an international operations office in Paris. . . . We also have joint agreements with Bristol in England (Bristol-Aerojet) and Orion in Germany (Orion-Aerojet).
>
> Hence there are no subsidiaries. Division managers are called to headquarters for a yearly meeting on international operations. International matters are handled as part of the agenda in the regular weekly corporate management meetings as required. The senior vice president and his corporate director of international operations visit Europe once a year and meet with executives of companies interested in association with Aerojet.

An electronics manufacturer said:

> Subsidiary executives visit headquarters when requested, in most cases at least once a year. However, the larger subsidiaries probably visit New York once each quarter. New York headquarters executives travel approximately 30 to 40 percent of the time

to visit the country and area headquarters, which is probably equal to four or five trips a year.

The policy at Procter and Gamble states that the top executive of the subsidiary is to visit headquarters every year. D. F. Howe, manager of the international division's personnel department, said that, in addition, key management people of the subsidiary visit headquarters at the time of the annual meeting and on a quadrennial basis. Visits occur at other times as the occasion demands. There is no set schedule for visits by headquarters executives to the subsidiary, but these do take place on a more or less regular basis.

Libbey-Owens-Ford has a different policy, as Vice President E. M. Everhard disclosed:

> We do not think it is too important for subsidiary executives to come to headquarters, although this is desirable. Contact from this office to our subsidiaries varies, but in the case of our Canadian subsidiaries it is a minimum of every three months.

Carnation Company's practice was explained by Vice President C. G. Todd:

> Ordinarily, a subsidiary executive will not come to the headquarters in Los Angeles more than once every three to five years. However, each officer of the foreign division's headquarters usually visits the subsidiaries two or three times a year.

The tire company executive said that his firm has no set formula for visits from subsidiary executives: "I would surmise that each top subsidiary executive comes into headquarters about once a year."

One visit a year is typical. An exception is American Standard, whose subsidiary executives visit headquarters three or four times a year and whose subsidiaries are visited every month. Libbey-Owens-Ford and Carnation reported less frequent visits.

Elserino Piol, of Olivetti, described his company's practices:

> Depending on the size and importance of the subsidiary, we visit very small subsidiaries at least once a year, and the most important ones once every two or three months. Visits from headquarters are on a nonscheduled basis according to necessity.

Pier A. Abetti, having worked for two leading American corporations abroad, was able to discuss both. When asked how often subsidiary executives visited headquarters, he replied:

> Very seldom in Univac, several times a year in General Electric. Many subsidiary executives are not asked, but they go to headquarters on their own initiative, for particular purposes, or just to find out what is going on.

Coordinating Communication

At Beckman Instruments, the organizational structure of the company serves as a pattern for coordinating communication. Details about the specific persons who provide this coordination have already been discussed in the section "Persons Who Communicate." A centralized mail service and communications center provides economies of consolidation in the transmittal of messages and information.

At Hughes International, specific communications at management levels—mentioned previously—are not always coordinated, but transactions between Hughes Aircraft Company and its affiliates are generally coordinated by the joint venture and license administration department. The men in this department are in constant communication with the Hughes technical people and with the technical and administrative personnel of the joint venture or licensee.

R. L. Michelson, of Honeywell, commented that communication usually occurs between persons holding similar positions with similar responsibilities, so that each is familiar with the other's day-to-day problems. Even if they work in different countries, they "talk the same language."

Even within divisions, specialists who are experts in their fields can communicate intelligently with anyone who has some technical knowledge and wants to communicate. Such people usually receive all inquiries relating to their specialties; even letters addressed to someone else are forwarded to them.

An executive of a leading computer company remarked: "Communications from the field in the United States are sent to headquarters abroad; therefore, the field abroad gets them days, sometimes even weeks, later." Another computer executive remarked about his company's coordination of communication: "It is left to individuals at the various locations, with the company encouraging close cooperation throughout its organizational setup." Company *A*'s executive had this to say:

> Each function is responsible for the coordination of its own communications. Companywide communications are coordinated prior to release by the sponsoring function—personnel policies by the personnel people, marketing policies by the marketing people, accounting instructions by finance, and so forth. Each letter of instruction or policy is assigned a number, and periodically numerical listings are sent to the countries to verify that they have received the information. However, general or individual management letters do not have numerical control unless it is established by a particular manager or function.

Responses of other companies lead one to conclude that in matters relating to the coordination of communication one must simply take things as they come. A few of these comments follow:

- Our only coordination of communications occurs when mail to various locales is grouped together in our mail room and sent out in bulk.
- Communications are coordinated by our message center, which handles incoming/ outgoing cables and mail. Of course, communications are also coordinated by top executives when they are discussing specific operations.
- Communications are not formally coordinated. Obviously, when the U.S. sales manager communicates with a subsidiary sales executive, there is no need for coordination.
- Many communications are coordinated and specified by standards that are laid down.

Causes of Communication Barriers

In the opinion of Dr. Ballhaus, of Beckman Instruments, the fundamental barriers to international communication seem to be distance, time, and local customs. A person's interpretation of a message, whether oral or written, is related to his total background, experience, and way of life. Even people trained to communicate in a common language find that their words have different connotations, depending on each person's temperament, education, experience, and social and economic heritage.

Nationals employed by foreign subsidiaries find it easy to communicate with people in their own organizations and internal operations, said Dr. Ballhaus, but they experience difficulty in communicating with executives of the parent organization. On the other hand, expatriates communicate more effectively with people in the parent company, but generally are handicapped in their day-to-day activities.

Dr. Ballhaus pointed out that some communications can be effective only if the persons involved can sit down together, visually demonstrate an item, and exchange questions and answers. The time and cost of international travel greatly restrict the frequency and duration of this type of direct communication. Consequently, the majority of communications are handled by the much less effective written medium. And Dr. Ballhaus concluded, "More use of direct visits and oral and visual communication appears to be the best method of reducing communication barriers."

R. W. Lindgren, of Hughes International, remarked that language remains a significant problem in international communication, although the use of linguistically qualified executives on both sides helps to alleviate this barrier. He said:

A problem associated with language is the difference in business practices and particularly in accounting techniques between countries. Therefore, efforts are made to standardize procedures between companies in order to avoid misunderstanding and confusion.

Millard Pryor, vice president of Singer, maintained that the major cause of communication barriers is distance and, with it, the inability of individuals to meet face to face. He said that in many companies no specific thought is given to overcoming this problem, even though they make certain that instructions are carried out and that information about the subsidiaries is always reviewed.

In a *Harvard Business Review* article, Mr. Pryor pointed out that, because international activities are complex, companies are limited on the amount of detailed planning they can undertake for their overseas operations. He commented further:

> The development of individual goals and strategies for an international company's entire overseas operations is a gigantic task, which, if formulated solely at the corporate headquarters level, would require a planning department staffed with personnel paralleling all the company's key overseas managers. Furthermore . . . there are certain major activities that cannot be properly planned outside the local environment. . . .*

Distance, languages, customs, ways of doing business must not only be accounted for but also abbreviated and interpreted to provide a continuing picture of significant events. As a rule of thumb, one can calculate the amount of information necessary to build a picture of a company's management and of its local situation. But obtaining such information is not easy; communication requirements are tough and the rate of information exchange slow.

One condition that creates one-dimensional solutions is relying too much on a single medium. One executive said: "It is our opinion that in this age of communication there are very few barriers to good communication with men in the field. Telephone, cables, and airmail have reduced all of the old barriers."

Another executive commented: "Poor communication is usually the result of inability to write clearly, combined with the writer's lack of forethought or his failure to put himself in the position of the recipient." Thus the message is as important as the medium, and improvement of only one of them is not enough to remove a barrier,

---

* Millard H. Pryor, Jr., "Planning in a Worldwide Business," *Harvard Business Review*, January–February 1965.

let alone reduce the colossal difficulties that exist in international communication.

Even in an age of unprecedented electronic marvels, the mechanics of communication may sometimes be stuffed with obsolete gear, and advanced information systems may become moribund. The author was told of delays in airmail delivery that lasted a fortnight in certain countries.

Anyone who has been exposed to the way telephones work in certain countries knows that they are sometimes nothing more than a joke. An international executive who has spent his career working in Latin American countries remarked that the great cost and low efficiency of telephone communications are often the result of faulty lines, but he added:

> I often spend twice as much time on the telephone as I should because I don't understand what the other person said in the first place. Everybody in this office has had the same experience. Repeatedly we have to ask: "What?" And if we use telegrams, we have to wait three days for the cable to be delivered.

These conditions are not universal; they exist in Central and Latin America and Asia but not in Europe. Most U.S. companies normally use airmail for their European communications since the time from mailing to receipt is approximately four days. Allowing another four or five days for the recipient to obtain an answer, write a letter, and have it typed and mailed back requires another four days; so the entire transaction takes from 12 to 14 days. Of course, more time is required if the recipient is out of the office, or if holidays or long weekends occur during this period.

All told, much can be said to support the thesis made by Procter and Gamble, Singer, and other companies that the main cause of the communication barrier is the difficulty of having face-to-face discussion and that the best solution is to have frequent meetings. But some companies that participated in this study do not subscribe to this solution because of the cost.

Less defensible, of course, are two opinions expressed by a minority of companies—that headquarters senses no stumbling block in communication or that it sees the stumbling block, but chooses to consider it unimportant or to deny its existence. For example, a leading corporation admitted that it has a communication barrier, but expressed reluctance to try to overcome it, citing the need for written communications that travel back and forth overseas and comparing this method favorably with walking next door to communicate and picking up the telephone and talking directly. However, the participating executive also added that written communications depend largely on the individual communicators and their ability to express themselves.

Executives in other companies cited some additional causes:

- Apart from distance, which constitutes a physical communication barrier, the main cause is the different environments in which subsidiaries operate. (Olivetti)
- One of the main causes of the communication barrier appears to be individual interpretation. This can be further complicated by time lags that occur when factual information is not received by the proper parties. (Company A)
- Communication barriers are caused by differences in national outlook, customs, and language. (Company B)

An experienced American executive said that international companies are "long in cash but short in ideas." This may seem cynical, but he and other executives have every right to expect more imaginative solutions to communication problems from most companies, especially those that are attempting to advance frontiers of knowledge.

3. The Selection and Use of Media

COMPANIES THAT WANT TO make breakthroughs in international communication need to take a long, cool look at the whole situation, including the state of the art and science of communication. Contrary to what many people believe, the current state does not lend itself to a solution through the rapid adoption of sophisticated approaches. One company, for example, assigned a seasoned systems analyst to study its worldwide communication problems and to develop a model communication system that could be applied to all the company operations abroad. The analyst spent two years on the project, visited several overseas locations, spoke at length with the executives in charge, and finally gave up. He commented on his experience:

I tried to develop a model communication system that would cut red tape to a minimum and increase efficiency throughout the international operations of our company's network. But, somehow, I got lost in the labyrinth of fences built by the different executives. As it turned out, our company's multinational organizational structure was not a carefully thought out proposition but an amalgamation of superimposed relationships.

Roland Grassberger, of Honeywell Venezuela, was of the opinion that communication should not be treated as one package. He said that all the problems he had encountered in his professional experience tended to vary by area.

In his most recent assignment, South America, Mr. Grassberger found conditions very different from those he had previously found in Europe. To cite just one example, Spanish is spoken in all Latin American countries except Brazil, but most educated men there also speak English. In business, English is generally accepted as the *lingua franca,* though foreign executives are better off if they can speak Spanish. Of course, in Europe many languages are spoken. By contrast, communications equipment in Latin America is far below the standard equipment in Europe. Also, in Latin America, even though distances are greater, transportation is more difficult. Europe is unquestionably superior in its technology.

Mail, The Three T's, and Meetings

Abundant use is made of the telephone, telegraph, and telex for communications purposes. Often, proximity makes the cost of communication by telephone cheaper and hence more advisable. It also increases the frequency of personal meetings. In addition, proximity increases the likelihood that the local executives in a foreign country will speak the language of the country where the parent company is situated.

Other things being equal, an American company's operation in Mexico encounters fewer communication problems than its subsidiary in Greece. Similarly, a German company's subsidiary in Italy has fewer communication problems than its factory in Brazil. This is not to say that the farther a subsidiary is from the parent company, the more likely it is to get the thin end of the communication stick. But distance can magnify communication barriers that are not spotted when the subsidiary is next door.

It cannot be repeated too often that the main problem facing an international company is judging the degree of communication that is appropriate for the specific people and organizations. The penalties for erroneous judgment can be particularly sharp. This is as true of the overall volume of communications as it is of the relative volume of the various media; namely:

- Mail (correspondence and reports).
- Telephone, telegram, and telex.
- Meetings of headquarters and subsidiary personnel.

In volume, mail takes the lion's share of communications. But no senior executive at home or abroad considered mail the most effective means. Harry B. Willis, Singer's general manager for Panama and Central America, commented:

The fact that the big bulk of communications is correspondence is not accidental. Costs make this mandatory in all cases where no real emergency exists. But productivity requires faster communication channels, and this is where the conflict comes in.

During a meeting in San Francisco, J. Gallo, assistant vice president of the international department, Bank of America, stated that, to help ease communication problems, the bank uses long-distance telephone calls, through intercom units, for meetings involving senior executives. The bank has a direct telex line to its subsidiaries in London and Mexico City. Furthermore, its policy requires the chief of international operations to travel abroad 70 percent of his time, while the administrative vice president is to hold one-day meetings with the key branches every year and rotate his meetings with the other branches so that

he visits all of them during a three-year period.

Because international operations have expanded so rapidly, visiting overseas branches and subsidiaries has become a major problem. Two months prior to the author's visit, the Bank of America had 40 branches. At the time of the meeting in San Francisco, the number had jumped to 52, half of the increase resulting from acquisition of Chile's Banco Italiano. Other participating companies reported rapid expansion, but none of them, financial or industrial, had a quantitative estimate of the increase in communications costs that had resulted from the increase in foreign subsidiaries and branches, even though their use of media had changed. Often, an important new project brought about a shower of telex messages. Said the director of a subsidiary that was about to build a new local factory:

We always check communications costs in our budget, but with a big operation like this, money ceases to be the barrier that it is under ordinary conditions. Nevertheless, we are careful to keep this expense under a separate account. For ordinary business conditions we have a budget of less than three thousand dollars per year for communications. This does not allow much telephoning or telegraphing.

Some companies have taken relatively stern financial control measures regarding their communications. But, because so many facets have not been studied and hence are uncontrollable, the success of these measures can be only relative. An area general manager remarked:

Significantly, while our own people observe the guidelines and try to reduce the amount of money spent on cables and long-distance calls, our dealers do not follow the same pattern. They tend to send more cables. And they expect a cable or call in return. Over a period of time, this tends to upset our communications budgets.

Another area general manager made the point that executive time should be counted in computing communications costs. This would upset several assumptions about the cost of different communications media. When the manager was asked what percentage of his company's communications were transmitted by the various media, he commented:

> I have not figured out any percentages. But we do spend a hell of a lot of time reading what comes in and answering requests. Even though executive time is a more expensive item than a stamp or a telephone bill, it is rarely appreciated as such.

The larger the company, the greater the likelihood that it has a complete and thorough communications network. R. N. Stevens, director of personnel, General Motors Overseas Operations, stated that all overseas plants are connected by telex, and telephone communications can be made quickly when necessary. There is also a constant flow of executives from the home office visiting overseas plants and overseas plant executives visiting the United States to fulfill the needs of the business.

In response to questions about the frequency and scope of meetings, Mr. Stevens drew from his desk an eight-page schedule on executive travel for a one-week period. In all, approximately 80 men were involved. About 50 executives of foreign nationality were visiting the United States. Twenty more were foreign executives expected to arrive within a fortnight. The rest were American executives traveling abroad.

The use of the telephone, telegram, and telex sometimes follows a developmental pattern that parallels a company's pattern of growth. This was the opinion of the personnel executive of the international division of a leading corporation:

> Our life, when we started overseas operations some 50 years ago, was based on cables. Since cables were expensive at the time, we used a code book. In those days, letters took ten days.

> But now that communications media have become so easy, one has to guard oneself. Expense is not the only factor. The temptation is always great that headquarters will become too involved in running the foreign subsidiaries.

Other Media

At American Motors International the following memos and forms are sent through the pipeline of correspondence:

- Interdepartmental letters.
- Speedimemos (see Exhibit 1).
- Action memos (see Exhibit 2).
- Requisitions for office supplies, reproduction, and printing.
- Mail orders.
- Export car orders.
- Automotive technical service bulletins (export).
- International built-in car orders.
- Monthly car sales and stocks on hand.
- Monthly production and car sales reports.
- Yearly distributor facilities reports.

Business opportunity reports are not included because, at American Motors, business opportunity is the responsibility of the regional sales director. How closely his work is coordinated with headquarters depends on a number of factors, one of which is the nature of the product itself. Automobiles and automotive products have an extremely

EXHIBIT 1. *Speedimemo (American Motors Corporation)*

SENDER:
1. DETACH SECOND COPY
2. SEND FIRST AND THIRD COPIES TO PERSON ADDRESSED

RECIPIENT:
1. WRITE REPLY AT BOTTOM
2. RETAIN FIRST COPY AND RETURN THIRD TO SENDER

REFER TO

☐ YOUR ☐ MY
☐ LETTER ☐ MEMO
☐ SPEEDIMEMO ☐ TELEGRAM
☐ PHONE CALL ☐ CONFERENCE
☐

OF (DATE) _____

AMERICAN MOTORS – SPEEDIMEMO

TO _____ ADDRESS _____

FROM _____ ADDRESS _____

SUBJECT _____ DATE _____

MESSAGE

_____

_____

_____

_____

_____

_____

ORIGINATOR-DO NOT WRITE BELOW THIS LINE   SIGNED _____

REPLY

_____

_____

_____

_____

_____

ADDRESS _____   SIGNED _____   DATE _____

RECIPIENT

long turnaround since they may be three years in development and the profit margins are generally low. These factors influence management decisions about the delegation of authority and structuring of the international organization, as well as its decisions about coordination and communications matters. Regional directors are required to visit each territory three or four times per year and, on the basis of their observations during these visits, to develop opportunity reports.

Companies with product lines that are more sensitive to minute ups and downs in the market and have substantially greater profit margins tend to develop business opportunity research teams. These teams conduct research on predetermined opportunity targets; consequently, their reporting practices differ from those of a departmental director or manager.

Correspondence practices of companies also vary widely. A major West Coast financial corporation used the same letter and report forms, and followed the same procedures, in communicating with its interna-

Exhibit 2.   *Action Memo (American Motors Corporation)*

ACTION MEMO
AMERICAN MOTORS

TO: _____

☐ PLEASE HANDLE   ☐ NOTIFY ME OF ACTION TAKEN
☐ REPLY—YOUR SIGNATURE   ☐ COPY TO ME
☐ FOR YOUR INFORMATION AND   ☐ RETURN   ☐ FILE   ☐ CIRCULATE
☐ PLEASE SEE ME
☐ PLEASE COMMENT
☐ REPLY—MY SIGNATURE
☐ FOR YOUR APPROVAL
☐ FOR YOUR SIGNATURE
☐ REWRITE AS INDICATED
☐

REMARKS:
_____

_____

_____

_____

_____

_____

_____

_____

_____

_____

_____

_____

_____

SIGNATURE	DATE	FOLLOW-UP DATE

FROM DEPARTMENT AND/OR LOCATION

tional subsidiaries that it used at head-quarters and in the country of origin. But a vice president commented:

> These forms and procedures did not answer the needs abroad. They were very rarely compatible with local practices; as a result, a whole new set of memos and report forms had to be designed for use abroad.

Expense account forms have been an item of major concern to international companies. In the course of this study, the author found that the forms of one company were usually incompatible with those of another; and, in a few instances, the forms and practices of one subsidiary differed from those of another in the same company. Of all the expense account forms, one type seemed to have greater merits. It was a version of a form used by an international consulting firm and amended slightly for its own associates. (See Exhibit 3.)

Company newsletters, field-use letters, and formal departmental letters are well-established methods of communication. They constitute a company's regular, continuing efforts to inform its men abroad about activities and developments in the organization. Magazines and bulletins are also used to keep overseas personnel abreast of organizational changes in the company, new facilities and products, application breakthroughs, and other changes. The following examples of such communications were provided by participating companies:

- American Motors' "Special Bulletin," which is sent to all Rambler international distributors.
- Honeywell's International Division bulletin, and its magazine, *The Honeywell World.*
- Goodyear's *Orbit,* a magazine with circulation both inside and outside the

company, which describes the world-wide interests and scope of Goodyear International Corporation.

- Goodyear's *GIC Newsletter,* distributed to GIC Americans working in Akron, Ohio, and throughout the world.
- Goodyear's *Quota,* published for international sales forces around the world.
- Goodyear Japan's quarterly magazine, published for dealers and employees to keep them informed of developments, and its news bulletin, published between issues of the magazine.

An executive of a leading Italian international combine, operating in electronics, rubber, and other fields, described how two types of information are channeled multinationally within his group:

1. *Information of a general nature.* This includes data, comments, and special studies made by the heads of the group. Information of common interest is circulated in periodical or occasional bulletins issued by the personnel department, the department for economic studies, the press and publicity department, and others. A three-month global report is provided by the central secretary's office for the heads of the company's affiliates operating abroad.

2. *Technical or specialized information.* Its circulation varies according to the nature of the information and the purpose for which it is required. Circulation of general and specific information among the managerial staff of the international group is insured by the frequent trips of the officers of the various services. In addition, management staffs of all the organizations throughout the world attend a conference held each autumn at the head office of the parent company so that they can thoroughly discuss important issues that affect the life of the company.

International company magazines and

Exhibit 3. *Expense Report (International Consulting Firm)*

EXPENSE REPORT

NAME (PRINT)

SEND REMITTANCE TO

CURRENCY | RATE OF EXCHANGE | PERIOD ENDED | CASH DUE (A)

DAY	PLACE	HOTEL (DAILY)	MEALS NO. AMOUNT	CAR & TAXI	LAUNDRY & VALET	CABLE TEL. & TEL.	TRANS-PORTA-TION	MISCELLANEOUS ITEM	AMOUNT	TOTAL CASH EXPENSE
1	16									
2	17									
3	18									
4	19									
5	20									
6	21									
7	22									
8	23									
9	24									
10	25									
11	26									
12	27									
13	28									
14	29									
15	30									
	31									

TOTALS →

PURCHASES ON YOUR AIR TRAVEL CARD (B)

AMOUNT	TICKET NUMBER	JOB NO.	ROUTING

B →TOTALS

REIMBURSABLE EXPENSE ALLOWANCE

REDUCE BY COST-OF-LIVING PAYMENT BY SUBSID. IF APPLICABLE

TOTAL CASH DUE (A)

AIR TRAVEL EXPENSES (B)

TOTAL EXPENSE FOR PERIOD (C)

COMPUTATION OF COST-OF-LIVING ALLOWANCE

COMMENTS

SIGNATURE

DISTRIBUTION OF TOTAL EXPENSES (C)

SUBSIDIARY OR ACCOUNT	JOB OR ACCT.	OUT-OF-POCKET EXPENSES, INCLUD-ING AIR TRAVEL	REA ALLOCATION	TOTAL EXPENSES

TOTAL EXPENSES FOR PERIOD

COPIES

ORIGINAL TO ACCOUNTING (SEND ON LAST DAY OF MONTH)

DUPLICATE TO REGIONAL OFFICE

TRIPLICATE TO IMMEDIATE SUPERVISOR

PLEASE INSURE THAT

(1) All incurred expenses are allocated to jobs or accounts.

(2) All totals are cross-footed.

(3) Documentation is attached.

(4) All air travel data are filled in.

(5) Rate of exchange is set out.

bulletins are usually well-written and well-edited printed publications. But they have one major shortcoming: Too often, they arrive too late to be of much value. Informal information channels (namely, international grapevines) have already carried the information. Whether the grapevines bring accurate information is another matter. What is significant is that the information has already been received and the receiver has already reacted to it.

The Banco Nacional de Mexico, a financial institution with multinational operations, used to send newspapers from Mexico City to its executives stationed abroad. The idea was that, after the executive read the news of financial, governmental, and industrial interest, he could pass the paper on to his wife so that she could read about social events. Long delays in the delivery of these newspapers killed the practice. Now the bank sends only clippings about financial matters.

Some international executives expressed the opinion that company newsletters and employee magazines channeled into the international pipeline are nothing more than an extension of the stuff used at home. But the persons who read the publications at home are a homogeneous group, while the persons who receive them abroad are not. Furthermore, many of these publications are not translated, and those that are very often have subject matter that was written for only one group.

The use of chartrooms for international industrial operations seems to have little popularity among executives abroad. Although a few examples of company chartrooms have been well publicized, little is known about developmental efforts of companies that were overzealous. These firms have been unable to obtain the results they hoped to gain and—for no apparent reason—have not improved their communication significantly. Some companies have even found their communication more blurred than it was previously.

In one company that was visited, the director of planning had made a very substial investment in a chartroom and had three assistants fully occupied with keeping it updated. The coverage of this chartroom was worldwide. But company executives found its value almost insignificant; and, when the director moved out of the planning job, his successor disposed of the room, its charts, and its specialists the very moment he took office.

Any study of communication has to include some discussion about language. International companies differ in their viewpoints and practices. Some prefer that only one language be used for letters and reports throughout the corporate worldwide network—the preferred language being the company's own country-of-origin language. There is some evidence that this practice is very effective.

Another possibility would be to use a standard language for all international business correspondence. Many European executives privately expressed the opinion that English is the number one language for this type of communication. For cables and telexes, country-of-origin languages are preferred.

Several American companies have established a practice followed by companies in Switzerland, Sweden, and other European countries—they require that their executives have the faculty of correspondence in at least two languages. An executive of a Midwestern electronics firm stated that, in its international communications, at least one of the correspondents often communicates in a second language. However, he added:

English has become the business language, and we have not experienced any real difficulty except in a few remote countries where command of the English language is limited. We are almost never required to translate letters or hire interpreters.

Similar responses were given by executives of other companies. These men, who are in a good position to know, do not believe that language is a major stumbling block. Two of these executives made the following comments:

- There is no language problem that we are aware of, since all international correspondence is in English. Within country borders, the local language is normally used.

- Language does not present a serious barrier because English is accepted as the common language. In addition, most executives are fluent in a second language, such as French, German, Spanish, or Portuguese.

The second comment refers to executives assigned overseas. Few companies would disagree that, even if English is a common language, international executives should speak the language of the country to which they have been assigned.

Emphasis on the use of English has resulted, not so much from spontaneity or popularity, as from corporate policy and procedures. As a corporate policy, it is considered reasonably efficient and has encountered relatively little adverse reaction compared with other corporate policies that have originated at headquarters. Policy on language sometimes goes much further. Several American corporations required that their Latin American subsidiaries correspond with one another in English because their headquarters received copies of all correspondence between these subsidiaries.

Closely related to language is the use of symbols. Typical responses were provided by two executives:

- The use of symbols depends on the country. If we are writing to France about financial matters, we refer to French francs; if we write to Germany, German marks; and to England, British pounds. Most of the devices we manufacture for use overseas refer to the metric system when measurements are involved.

- We generally use foreign monetary symbols when corresponding with our foreign subsidiaries and for other foreign correspondence. The determining factor is the nature of the correspondence. However, we do use the English system rather than the metric system when referring to measurements in our correspondence.

Case Studies on Media Use

The reaction of key executives to the correspondence and general communications load has been that it provides excellent documentation that organizations are too defensive. This opinion was both a general complaint and a self-criticism. Senior men said that they and their colleagues are caught in the trap of thinking that the more they write, the better they are covered. Another major reason for the communications jungle, they said, is inertia.

What is often forgotten is the ironical fact that the communications jungle itself gives a man the feeling that he has accomplished an honest day's work. A Mexican executive provided additional insight about communications:

There is something wrong with the way headquarters plays the standards for evaluating performance. In our particular case, New York asks for results, and the executive working abroad has to show results. But not every day can one come up with something terrific to satisfy increasingly stiff criteria. Hence the foreign executive who does not have results to show makes up for the lack of them with correspondence, cables, and calls.

Company F, a leading American electronics and business equipment firm, established solid foundations for a worldwide empire throughout the postwar years. At the time of this study, over 30 percent of its business came from abroad. The following figures show the percentage of time spent by one of the subsidiaries in communicating with the international headquarters and the regional headquarters through the three types of media—mail; telephone, telegram, and telex; and personal meetings:

International HQ		*Regional HQ*
Mail	80%	48%
TTT	10%	22%
P.M.	10%	30%

A significant factor was that the subsidiary and its regional headquarters were in the same city, only 300 meters from each other. Still, an impressive amount of communication was done by mail, even though subsidiary personnel could have used the telephone or walked down the street for a meeting. Furthermore, 2 percent of the TTT communications were being handled by telex, although it would seem that in this case telex would not have been used at all.

Knowledgeable executives in this firm, and in others, suggested that interoffice correspondence between departments and other company units situated in the same city be limited to letters and memos required for documentation. However, this is rarely the case. Said one senior executive:

> During the first five months of this year my department registered 800 letters as outgoing mail. The general manager's office registered 380 letters during the same period. These are original letters, and we don't count copies. If we did, the statistics would have made depressive reading, since in our company everybody copies everybody else.
>
> Incoming mail is a totally different affair. On a daily basis, my department gets an average of 45 letters from the regional headquarters alone. The general manager gets 60 to 80 letters daily. This includes the copies. On the average these figures represent between two-thirds and three-fourths of the load.
>
> It should be evident that if I wish to do a good job along the lines of my main functions, I just don't have the time to handle all this mail, much less answer it intelligently.

Company G, an overseas banking group, reported that the media used for communications with international headquarters were 90 percent mail, 9 percent TTT, and 1 percent personal meetings. The subjects covered by these categories were as follows: 60 percent financial information, 10 percent personnel matters, and 30 percent other matters.

Much of what is included in the "other" category concerns communications necessary to answer specific questions. For example, in some Latin American countries government reports on business statistics are too vague and too slow for the business community. Hence the bank must send headquarters a monthly report describing prevailing economic conditions, in addition to the usual financial reports on loans and other business matters.

Company H, the Mexican subsidiary of a European company, reported that its communications with headquarters were as follows: 90 percent mail, 6 percent TTT, and 4 percent meetings. The 6 percent TTT are primarily telegrams and, secondarily, telex. The use of the telephone is contrary to company policy. Country-of-origin executives normally visit the subsidiary three or four times a year, while subsidiary executives visit headquarters about three times/persons per year (a total of three visits made by one, two, or three executives). The six key men of the subsidiary were all country-of-origin Europeans; they included the general manager, the assistant general manager, and the directors of marketing, personnel, finance, and manufacturing.

The weekly incoming mail was approximately a hundred letters. Much of the correspondence was addressed to the general manager, but it also included factory correspondence as well as administrative, personnel, and sales mail. There was little correspondence with other corporate operations in the Western Hemisphere; it constituted only about 10 percent of the outgoing mail, which was at a level slightly below that of the incoming mail.

Company I, a chemical company in Nicaragua working through licensing and marketing agreements with American chemical companies, found that cables can be used to best advantage for exceptions, confirmation of prices, arrivals, deliveries, and so on. Thus the greatest bulk of the communications is correspondence and routine reports sent by mail. Communication with headquarters was as follows: 80 percent mail, 10 percent TTT, and 10 percent personal meetings.

The company had three types of personal meetings:

- Technical visits involving all matters relating to plant procedures, laboratory tests, observance of specifications, and quality control.
- Sales visits, which varied in frequency and nature with the seasons since the company's business is agricultural chemicals.
- Management visits, which center on the broader directives, investments, ef-

ficiency measures, and other aspects of management.

The sales manager of this company stated that his problem with correspondence is that it takes too long to be useful. The mail does not seem to go through. Express airmail from New York takes six days, and from Managua to Nicaragua's second city it takes ten days or more. Then there is the problem of semantics. Two Nicaraguan executives commented that, as far as they are concerned, the international corporations with which they work through licensing agreements have shown much more awareness about the semantics of their communications than local firms, even those that are family-owned.

In Company J, area management reported that communications with international headquarters at the home office, and with the branch offices and subsidiaries, were 85 percent mail, 10 percent TTT, and 5 percent meetings. Said the general manager:

> Our main problem with mail is obtaining fast answers. Not only are there great delays in mail delivery, but between the time headquarters receives the mail and answers it, from two to four weeks usually pass. For various reasons this is too long a delay, and cables and telephone calls become necessary to expedite the correspondence. A result: our bills go up.

Company K, an American subsidiary in Panama, provided the following statistics for communications under "ordinary business conditions": 89 percent mail, 10 percent TTT, and 1 percent personal meetings.

The small percentage of personal contacts represented the few days the area manager spent in Panama and the day or so the subsidiary general manager spent at headquarters. Telex was used much more in this company than in other participating companies.

Company L, the subsidiary of an American electronics combine, uses the mail for 95 percent of its communications and telephone, telegram, and telex for almost 5 percent. The percentage of meetings is insignificant. The general manager said that telegraph bills have been increasing and telephone bills have continued to increase. He commented that, although business has also improved, "telephone bills somehow find a way to grow faster than business."

Personal conferences were discontinued by this general manager because he believes that they are primarily inspection visits, rather than a means of communicating. He said:

> Rare, indeed very rare, is the case where a headquarters executive visits us to explain and discuss a specific subject. Practically every visit takes the colors of control rather than communication. This is attested by the fact that all these visits have been inward-oriented, concerned with internal company matters. Yet, here at the operations level of the subsidiary, we feel that visits by headquarters executives should have been oriented in exactly the reverse direction—outward toward our customers.

The Application of Computers

As seen in some quarters, the use of computer systems analysis for solving international communication problems is not yet of age. In the author's opinion, the computer is out—for the time being at least —as a means of easing international communication problems. Executives of domestic operations, exposed to what the computer can and cannot do, recognize that the major difficulties and challenges emanate not so much from the machine itself as from pre-input and postoutput factors.

Uniformity is, of course, a major consideration of companies that are developing computer programs. Very often, achieving it requires rethinking and redesigning all a company's systems and procedures, in the course of which executives in the foreign subsidiaries may hear disturbing reports about developmental efforts at home. Elaborating on the value of uniformity in procedural matters is superfluous; its advantages have been known for years, both nationally and internationally. What must be said is that on the national scene the companies that are most highly computerized, with streamlined systems and procedures, have tightened up significantly and moved toward centralized control. Will this also happen internationally? Murmurings among subsidiary executives indicate that it may, for these reasons:

- The parent companies have assumed responsibility for systems and have been the principal suppliers of experienced systems manpower. They also have expressed intention to undertake foreign systems assignments.
- The parent companies have undertaken to hire and train a sufficient number of college graduates to meet both domestic and foreign forecast manpower needs in the data processing field. However, many subsidiary executives fail to realize that U.S. companies have difficulty meeting even their immediate manpower needs.
- The progress being made domestically indicates that greater centralized control is in sight, rather than a move in the opposite direction.
- Many companies are planning to establish interchangeable procedures that will permit them to move data between affiliates and domestic data banks and

make feasible a steadier application of financial controls.

"Not so," said R. W. Callon, Alcan's manager of systems development, about the increasing centralization. His data processing department has functional responsibility for the use of computers throughout Alcan Canada and, on request, provides in-house consulting services to group operating companies in England, Norway, Japan, and the United States, as well as for installations pending in Jamaica, Guiana, Australia, Germany, and other areas. Mr. Callon explained why he disagreed about centralization:

When we first considered the use of computers, there was a tendency to think of a highly centralized type of organization. Reasons for this were our less complicated business activities, higher hardware costs per unit of output, and the lack of realization about the difficulty involved in providing complete "clean" input for what is now often referred to as a data bank. With the passage of time and the benefit of experience, we shifted to a much more decentralized concept.

I think it is obvious that one cannot install an overall system in one global effort. It is simply too large a job because of the changes in management's needs. First one must do the most profitable subsystems, gradually merging these into an overall business information system. In doing this we must try to avoid being overly concerned with the automation of current data systems and make every effort to try to answer management's needs of tomorrow.

Discussions with L. C. Kuiken, manager of planning techniques and the data center of Shell in London, clearly illustrated the evolution of management policy on matters concerning computing machinery. This evolution was seen as a natural development for the multinational company that has to concern itself with relations between headquarters and the subsidiaries, at home and abroad, and intersubsidiary relations.

More than simple compatibility of equipment and interchangeability of programs is involved. Some basic policies have to be established. The company has to decide whether it wishes to do business with one computer manufacturer or with many. The former alternative has been practiced by many companies, but the author can find no grounds for it other than the mystical.

A few years ago, Shell decided to use one principal manufacturer, particularly for the smaller companies in the group. But management also concluded that the larger companies in the group needed more than one manufacturer to supply data processing equipment. Three fundamental reasons were behind this decision:

- More rational selection of equipment, since every manufacturer's equipment offers certain definite advantages for specific jobs.
- Getting out of the hands of one manufacturer and changing a basic supplier when new machines are introduced, in a reasonably smooth way, without upsetting transition.
- The unquestionably better services—both in systems and in maintenance—that manufacturers will give when they realize they do not have a monopoly within the customer company.

Another multinational oil company indicated that developing standardized methods of accounting and financial reporting on a worldwide basis required great effort and even an explicit statement from the board of directors. The major cause of the company's difficulty was executives' unwillingness to part with the time-honored profit-and-loss approach to decentralized operations. The challenge was combining effectiveness and flexibility in evaluating management by profit-and-loss criteria with uniformity in systems and procedures.

Profit-and-loss criteria provide an excellent basis for achieving efficiency, but some executives contend that standardization handicaps P & L implementation. Nevertheless, after the first pains of conversion, systems and procedures standardization on a global basis can help the top man of a subsidiary obtain financial results. Much of the argument about centralization and standardization actually hinges on delegation of authority and corporate policies that define "how far to go."

An international company with long experience in data processing has developed what it calls "integrated financial modeling." The task was complicated because of incompatibilities. According to the director of data processing, too many differences in systems and procedures make even the concept of a data bank a thing of the future. Said he: "We have to crawl before we can run."

Since this company has 14 operating subsidiaries, management estimates that standardization will take a long time, as will achieving homogeneity in processing financial data. Subsidiary executives say, not too loudly, that such homogeneity will eventually lead to standardization in decision making even if this was not intended during the early stages. Much depends on how corporate management sizes up the proposed changes in data collection, processing, and reporting.

An executive from a large multinational corporation commented that, when its top management evaluates the worldwide marketing network, it cannot determine overall optimum return-on-investment potential. The company has an annual budget of $600 million. Undoubtedly, it will try to discover the most efficient method of determining worldwide potential when mathematical and computational means make it feasible—if financial and operational standardization is established by then.

Professional trend watchers maintain that multinational data processing is not yet mature, and will not be mature for some time. Certain signs indicate that it may even take a reverse. Data automation has excited the imaginations of many executives at home and abroad, but in many countries where international companies operate the state of the art is some ten years behind that of the countries of origin. This discrepancy is just enough to make the subject controversial and to hamper efforts to expand the use of computer systems.

Headquarters executives share such thoughts with confidants, but cannot express them publicly because they humiliate executives abroad. Because headquarters cannot afford to put highly sophisticated computers into the subsidiaries, the discrepancy will probably continue for some time; and, as a consequence, systems and procedures between headquarters and subsidiaries will continue to lack homogeneity, even though the headquarters people want it.

This study fully documents that companies, even the more powerful ones, have neither the financial and economic incentive nor the trained specialists to proceed with worldwide streamlined computer systems. What they do have is concern for cost-effectiveness. At this time, the emphasis on cost-effectiveness precludes cross-continental computer networks. Esso had four computer centers in Scandinavia: a medium-size system in Stockholm and three small peripheral computers in Oslo, Copenhagen, and Helsinki. The Helsinki center had already changed to a third-generation machine when Esso Europe decided that all data processing should be concentrated in the Stockholm center—which had also changed to a larger, medium-scale, third-generation computer. The equipment in the three other centers was then dismantled. Cost-effectiveness, the author was told, was the moving gear behind the decision.

Computers installed in subsidiaries are not yet paying their way. Headquarters executives remarked that their companies are not getting the mileage they should get out of these systems. In the United States several large corporations decided to roll back the red carpet that they had laid for sophisticated computer gear and for teletransmission. This situation is surprisingly similar in European corporations and American companies in Europe.

In 1967 the Bank of America was in the process of a massive systems change, which systems analysis planning was directed to complete in 1972. During the early stages hardware changes were made. This involved the consolidation of twelve check centers (ERMA) and two general data processing centers into two integrated centers, each equipped with three large-scale systems. Most significant, the bank decided to keep on multiprogramming and to avoid core sweeping and other time-sharing exercises. As one of the executives explained:

The bank has chosen remote and delayed batch processing, with its applications running in four partitions: (1) an applications background, (2) a multiple-access foreground, (3) check-handling procedures, and (4) diagnostic exercises—an engineering checkup without interrupting the main structure.

In the new systems design, which involves a complete renewal of hardware, on-line transactions were eliminated because of their prohibitive cost. On-line status was retained, permitting automatic interrogation because it avoids plurality in printouts and is cost-effective.

What lies ahead in teletransmission and long-distance data processing will largely be dictated by communication developments. Communication costs today are too high and hence prohibitive to profit-minded companies. The vice president of a leading financial organization remarked that telecommunications are not needed in new systems design because, with strategically installed data centers, one can bring in bags filled with messages and have them processed in three to four hours. P. W. Weiser, director of executive development, Lockheed Missiles and Space Company, commented:

Communications, even within the continental United States, is a very perverse problem. It is not just a matter of speaking the same language. The problem is magnified in the international field, particularly since the need to take a systems look at major problems cannot be comprehended in some quarters.

Increasingly, industrial and financial organizations consider return on investment a criterion for judging the wisdom of their computer expenditures. In years past this was considered for the aggregate; now it is done on an application-by-application basis. In general, costs must be covered and some residue must be left. Much depends, of course, on what is meant by "savings." The meaning varies from company to company and from country to country. The fact that computer savings are so loosely defined is further proof that data processing in international business has not yet come of age.

4. Prevailing Communication Problems: Channels and Information

SENIOR INTERNATIONAL EXecutives who want better communication are usually willing to pay for it, even though the price is high. What companies seldom realize is that their present ineffective communication may be even more costly.

In 1966, when the author was conducting worldwide research for his AMA report, *Developing the International Executive,* he found that a majority of the participating executives—American, British, French, German, Italian, Swiss, Israeli, and Japanese—estimated that half of their time was devoted to communication with headquarters. More recently, a managing director stationed in Mexico said that he spends 80 percent of his time solving local personnel problems and resolving problems in consultation and communication with headquarters.

In the course of conducting this research, the author heard with an impressively high frequency complaints by overseas managing directors about the "blinders" worn by people at headquarters. Comments by the author about inefficient communication lines invariably produced this type of remark:

We have communication problems with our headquarters people and we tell them so, but they keep on arguing that all this is our imagination. They say that in reality there are no serious communication problems at all, or at least none of such magnitude that we should worry about them.

Long Channels and Excessive Quantity

Some international companies emphasize that information-dissemination techniques should be more than a one-way street with information moving in one direction. Subsidiaries require a continual flow of comprehensive and easy-to-digest data from headquarters, and headquarters needs feedback from the subsidiaries if both are to function appropriately. Variations in products, markets, locations, and numerous other factors complicate the communication picture and slow down the flow of information. However, emergencies are frequently routed straight to the top, rather than through usual channels, and sometimes bring about organizational catastrophies.

An example of a cumbersome system was provided by a multinational computer manufacturer. Until a few years ago, the inquiry of a customer in a European city, such as Düsseldorf, about a steel application in the United States had to go up and down the organizational ladder through 12 distinct steps. (See Exhibit 4.) Since the company's response had to follow the same route, as much as two or three months elapsed before the customer received an answer.

This type of communication conforms with traditional management theory. It is used by hundreds of companies because they believe that everyone up and down the structure should be informed about everything. The villain is not management theory as such but inappropriate application of that theory. Distance makes things difficult, but worse than distance is the unnecessary interposition of organizational levels in the middle of an information system.

As a consequence, some managing directors of foreign subsidiaries expressed resent-

Exhibit 4. *Routing of Customer Inquiry (International Computer Manufacturer)*

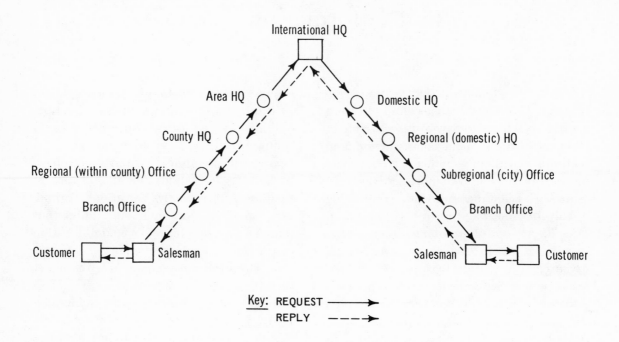

Key: REQUEST ⟶
      REPLY ⤍

ment about the multinational corporation's structure—the very organizational structure that makes American management strong at home. Guido L. Forgnoni, general manager of Univac's operations in Mexico, explained why executives have these negative reactions:

A great part of companies' strength in their domestic operations lies in the specialization of managerial functions. But this specialization can have ambiguous if not detrimental results in international operations. Highly specialized functions at headquarters are sometimes responsible for the fact that international executives receive contradictory orders. This situation occurs because the executives seldom know what someone else says or has written; and, when such a situation does happen, it is magnified by distance.

Slow action abroad often reflects a huge amount of red tape. For instance, there exist colossal problems in interpreting, administering, and applying the law in most foreign operations. This fact alone implies different solutions, applies different weights, and calls for different structures than those followed at home.

In the subsidiary of a participating company, two senior executives working in the same building and living in the same city were required to communicate through telex channeled through the headquarters. In the course of this study, the author was told of five similar examples, and all five of the participating executives commented that these communciation barriers were built to provide excuses for inactivity and avoidance of responsibility.

The personnel director of the Mexican subsidiary of an American corporation—a man seasoned in his job—expressed the opinion that an important factor underlying the increased volume of communications is "personal protection." Executives write letters and reports that are operationally useless because they believe that such correspondence helps them fulfill their responsibilities and demonstrates to others that they are alert and busy. The original correspondence builds fences around functional areas, and the copies to other persons reinforce the fences.

From Lebanon to Venezuela the author visited general managers of subsidiaries who receive ten inches of report requests per week—which they are expected to read, understand, evaluate, and answer. From this standpoint, headquarters executives are highly reluctant to devote their energies to unrealistic or idealistic efforts. They usually have more than enough essential activities to perform; namely: selecting reliable sources of information, checking the validity and credibility of this information, analyzing the information in the light of worldwide corporate objectives and policies, and supervising the circulation of information throughout the domestic and overseas operations.

This situation was summarized by M. Y. Yoshino, chairman of the international business and comparative management program, Graduate School of Business Administration, University of Southern California, Los Angeles, as follows:

> Excessive demand for information and reports not only has a demoralizing effect upon local executives, but it also diverts them from more pressing operating problems. Frequently, the headquarters staff are paralyzed by the sheer volume of information coming from foreign affiliates and fail to make effective use of it. Decisions are likely to be delayed, leading to losses in operating effectiveness.*

---

* M. Y. Yoshino, "Toward a Concept of Managerial Control for a World Enterprise," *Michigan Business Review*, March 1966.

Poor Quality of Information

Many firms expressed the opinion that this is their biggest single information problem. In some countries, international executives said, every source document needs to go through successive tests to insure dependability. Price levels, discount rates, product codes, and almost everything registered on an original document has to be tested.

Many senior executives abroad do not even know how much money they will get to run their shows until a number of reports have made the rounds of corporate offices. Furthermore, in many companies, when budgets are carried over from the domestic operations to international, nobody insures that the data they carry are dependable and that the information channels work properly. At times, plans are shaky because the forecast conditions on which they are based can move in almost any direction. Therefore, the international manager needs to learn about the varying degrees of undependableness in his budgets and plans. Otherwise, he will occasionally find himself building castles of sand. A considerable number of executives in foreign assignments, American as well as European, emphasized these basic facts of international life.

The conceptual framework for managing multinational operations has to include the whole spectrum of subjects concerning the activities of an industrial organization. For example, communication barriers have a bearing on engineering standards. Feedback from headquarters can act as a moving gear to guarantee uniform quality—if the engineering executive in charge realizes that in some countries quality often cannot be maintained.

The reasons for fluctuations in quality are varied. Materials are an important factor and local standards, even more important. In many countries both factors are a problem; in a few, neither is. Foreign executives identified Venezuela as an exceptional example. American and British companies are particularly comfortable there because Venezuela has streamlined its engineering work, and a number of Venezuelan engineers have been educated in North American universities. Said Roland Grassberger, of Honeywell Venezuela:

European nations have deep-rooted convictions about their standards. Some of them set standards to exclude foreign sources of equipment, rather than to facilitate work. This is not the case in Venezuela. When I compare my work here with what I was doing in Germany, I find that adjustment here was much easier.

Most efforts to achieve international standardization have failed. Because of these failures communication barriers are much more difficult than they need be. Furthermore, it is doubtful that any sharp changes will occur, although many small ones will probably take place. Small changes are easier to forecast and explain, as one industrial executive pointed out: "Because we have proceeded by making only small changes, we have gotten no negative comments on performance." Then he added, "But the increasing frequency of such changes may eventually make both local governments and our own headquarters change their minds."

Here again headquarters response is an important factor. Engineering executives commented that often the roots of design troubles can be found in the fact that a company thinks of a group of countries as one area with one situation. But this is fallacious because no two countries have the same engineering conditions. And even though marketing has other types of variables, marketing executives have also observed that

persons at headquarters tend to overgeneralize.

As a consequence, one of the international executive's concerns is obtaining from the realm of his operations sound documentation on variables highlighting similarities and differences and describing what effects they have on the company. This calls for far-ranging minds and communications channels of remarkable quality. It also necessitates that pitfalls be avoided, which is very difficult to do, especially in Europe. Succumbing to pitfalls occurs less often in Latin America because, as one senior executive pointed out, "The differences from country to country are so much more evident there."

International companies cannot conquer communication frontiers until they become more discerning about what they need and want, and establish suitable policies and procedures. By wanting the most of everything, they make it virtually impossible to handle the most important factor of all: obtaining reliable sources of information.

Lack of Feedback

Subsidiary general managers very often resent the too-frequent lack of reaction to information they transmit. Said the chief executive of an American subsidiary in Mexico:

It is our company's policy to forward an end-of-the-month marketing report to headquarters. In the three years I have been here, I never received any reaction, positive or negative, to the monthly reports I have sent. And I have started believing that headquarters rarely, if ever, reads these reports and never really carefully considers my comments. I doubt if I am asking too much when I expect my superiors to let me have their thoughts and their reactions.

The lack of feedback from headquarters was emphasized frequently by the executives who were interviewed. Men seasoned in international business remarked that in their judgment the purpose of international business information is to enable both the area manager and his subordinates abroad to make intelligent decisions. And, while the area manager needs information about all the functions under his authority, he should not bypass his basic responsibility of providing feedback to his subordinates who run the foreign subsidiaries.

One international manager cited the following example: His subsidiary needed to change a certain machine component within a reasonably short period of time. Although the change was minor, a request addressed by the general manager of the subsidiary to his immediate superior at the headquarters remained unanswered for two months. A second letter was sent and was followed by three more months of silence.

With these delays, the matter became urgent. The general manager telexed headquarters for immediate delivery. In reply he received a telex informing him that such matters were not the responsibility of "this office" but of "Mr. X"—an executive outside the authority of the regional director to whom the initial request had been addressed, but whose office was on the same floor in the same building as the director's office.

Since an effective reporting system reflects the needs of a particular business, it can obviously assume many different forms. The same is true of feedback. Nonetheless, the basic objective of both is to improve the management process. Feedback is a fundamental of many managerial activities—of planning the long-range development of subsidiaries, of formulating strategies to insure a high return on investment, of coordinating the execution of tactical moves to strengthen the company's competitive position in specific markets, of re-evaluating current programs and taking steps to correct problems, of controlling local operations, and of numerous other managerial activities.

When the general manager of a subsidiary abroad sends his report to headquarters, he is not looking for a verdict or for acceptance. What he hopes to obtain is some feedback that will enable him to do his job better. Such feedback requires centralized coordination. This can be done in many different ways, but the one preferred by most international companies is centralization under an area operating head. In some firms, field feedback is supervised by an administrative manager. Feedback is required by all managerial functions—marketing, production, engineering, and others—whether they are national or international.

In Tel Aviv, Sol Goodelman, of the Electronics Corporation of Israel, commented about the importance of industrial feedback to a nation:

> In Israel, the lack of major industrial activity inhibits the gaining of knowledge and skill during the transition process from R & D through production to field maintenance. In turn, this prevents the country from getting the industrial feedback it needs to develop additional industry.

Not only does lack of feedback handicap the men assigned abroad, but it also makes the headquarters executives seem that much more remote to the executives abroad. Inattention to reports from foreign subsidiaries blurs headquarters' view of international business opportunities. When practiced consistently, it affects the judgment of key men in the very areas for which they are responsible.

Few executives would suggest that difficulties result only from failure to provide feedback or to keep the pipeline open. Yet not one executive was able to make a straightforward defense of his company's failure to respond. Quite the contrary, many overseas executives said that a substantial number of their marketing problems result from headquarters' not being careful enough in planning for a new or expanding market and, surprisingly often, from headquarters' not using the information it asks the subsidiaries to submit. A seasoned international executive commented:

> It is my feeling that the men at headquarters are generally too remote to feel the impact and blow-by-blow development of daily activities at the subsidiary level.

> Quite often people from the head office travel around to put pressure on the local operating executives instead of serving as sensory elements. The result is that headquarters never gets out of its blind.

There is little doubt that over a period of time communication barriers can limit the expansion of international companies. One major deterrent is that industrial leadership has not yet made its weight felt internationally. Another factor, mentioned by some of the senior executives, is that the basic difficulties in structuring efficient communications networks can be traced to the weaknesses of the human race. One characteristic of human weakness is the tendency to secrecy. Another is that most men believe that their private squabbles and worries are important to the company's well-being and representative of its major difficulties. These factors can erode the best multinational information system, clog open channels, and curtail the establishment of future programs.

Seen in this light, the problem is one of setting up a worldwide communications network that will have an impact on the fundamentals of human nature. Even in the best of circumstances, such a program is grandiose, and grandiose programs always require great commitments of time, money, and human effort—which seems to form a somewhat vicious circle.

In some of the discussions key executives regretted the corrosive influence of "cosmetics in international communication." Their thesis was that too many messages have been coated with make-up. This practice was criticized, caustically at times, as a severe pitfall, as was the fact that few junior executives are taught how to perceive and formulate problems and how to set and present their aims and objectives. Said one senior man:

> I think that the development of a communications network and the international executives' role in it have been left in the wrong hands. From the beginning, communication should be studied from the systems approach. And the system is the man.

5. Prevailing Communication Problems: Management and People

ALTHOUGH IT IS POSSIBLE FOR headquarters and foreign subsidiary executives to have the same point of view and to agree about the implementation of policies and programs, it is not usual. The usual situation is that overcentralization and fixed patterns of decision making hamper operations abroad, as well as burden the communications network. Many decision-making patterns successfully followed in the United States are simply not applicable abroad. Insistence on their application in other countries creates adverse reaction and noise in the communications network.

Although subsidiary executives may react adversely to headquarters' advice, they seldom carry on a vendetta against it. Nor do they concentrate on staying in the middle of the road or performing a sort of balancing act with what they think right and what headquarters wants. Most subsidiary executives are primarily interested in doing an efficient job. This requires two-way intelligence. Foreign-based executives repeatedly said that they recognize their need for guidance. But a corporation should let an executive assigned abroad make some mistakes so that he will learn from them.

No foreign executives who were interviewed questioned the need for policy statements. Policies enable companies to manage by remote control—to coordinate the actions of decentralized units. But field executives question the lack of flexibility sometimes found within the policy framework.

This research documents that the bigger the company, the greater the likelihood that, because a centralized management philosophy prevails, headquarters will use fixed concepts and patterns in managing the subsidiaries. As one executive remarked, "If it weren't for all the stereotypes swinging down the organizational pipeline, a subsidiary's general manager might die of excitement when he gets news from the home office."

Country-of-origin nationals assigned abroad also tend to apply stereotypes learned at home. The risk is that rules and detailed methods valid in the country of origin are rarely valid in faraway lands. As an overseas manager admitted:

When you work for a big organization it is easier to follow general business habits, but eventually variation in the outside environment catches up with you. Environmental differences also affect your family. This will lead to frustration unless you are able to stand up and fight for your own position, and use your own best judgment.

Corporate Management and Control

The nature and magnitude of the communications vary with the amount of financial control exercised by the parent company. With extensive control, most communications are sent or received by headquarters. Because many top executives in the subsidiaries of such companies fully realize that this type of control is a way of corporate life, most of them accept it. But they resent many conditions that accompany it, such as the numerous unnecessary and probabilistic requests for information and the overcrowding of the communications channels.

Financial planning and budgets provide the necessary framework for management control. "But," commented the general manager of a subsidiary, "the original information is often as unreliable as a house of cards." He described his problem:

To develop a budget we need a marketing plan. This plan is based on the sales forecast, which varies considerably for different products and in different countries. But for products with advanced technology, plans have become quite unreliable, especially in their timing. A change in timing can ruin a marketing plan, which in turn blows all the budgetary fuses.

International executives with a keen sense of humor sometimes laugh at companies' assertions that tightening control improves profitability. Financial control can be distorted. Financial data and sales statistics can be meaningless out of context. Executives at headquarters can be so far removed from the reality of foreign operations that they might as well be managing fictitious subsidiaries.

Superimposed methods, systems, and procedures that are workable at home can knock against legal regulations and other requirements in foreign countries. For example, accounting practices vary from country to country to reflect business and tax regulations; therefore, accounting systems tailored for one country cannot be applied wholesale to another. Thus homogeneity of reporting on a worldwide basis is difficult, if not impossible, for most companies.

Tight control does not guarantee that local management will adhere to the headquarters' policies. Sometimes the pendulum even swings the other way, and implementation of rigid policies and standards by cor-

porate headquarters results in virtually no control over their foreign operations. Private, off-the-record discussions with headquarters and subsidiary executives confirmed this. Seasoned men reflected a shrewd awareness of the present situation and of difficulties still to be encountered in the control relationship.

Some companies are so overcentralized that one wonders why they pay their top men abroad $60,000 per year or more. The ceiling of local decisions seems to be so low that they probably could be made by men earning considerably less.

In one particular case, the parent company insisted on getting copies of bank reconciliations from all its affiliates. These statements were so varied and incomprehensible that the executives at headquarters could not even read them. Although the practice had become a joke throughout the organization, nobody tried to change it; some even threw away the unreadable statements for fear of repercussions.

Some situations mentioned by executives greatly surprised the author. He had not expected the magnitude and frequency of blind spots that he found in information systems designed for international industrial operations. Although many situations resulted from oversight or negligence, a few resulted from attempts to standardize communication policies and practices. Organizational wizards assigned to the task thought they had identified the communication bug, but their efforts to get rid of it were so catastrophic that even the profitability figures were affected.

An American company bought control of a family-owned Latin American firm that was making a healthy 20 percent return on investment. Much of the business came through tightly knit personal relationships between the owner of the firm—who was head of the family—and the customers' top executives. And, as is usual in many areas of the world, the firm did not conform to specific policies and practices. Family management often improvised, and it did so successfully.

The acquiring company, nonetheless, insisted on changing procedures to make them compatible with those prevailing at the headquarters organization. Theoretically, the move was sound, but in practice it was a disaster. Procedural changes brought about a tremendous increase in paperwork. Six clerks had to be hired to handle the onslaught of paper. The general manager (retained from the family management) had to divert his attention to communications and could no longer give personal attention to his customers. In two years, the 20 percent return on investment—the main reason the subsidiary had been purchased—shrank to a meager 6 percent.

Organizational needs of subsidiaries add to the challenging and complicated tasks of headquarters. The executives at headquarters must plan, coordinate, and control three organizational factors: product or product group, function, and geographical area. Eberhard Schmidt, general manager of the German Bovari Company, maintains that line authority follows geographic structure because the other types of structure are less suited to overall coordination. Whatever type of structure is used by a company, efficient coordination requires comprehension and teamwork on its upper levels.

International industrial enterprises have not yet found the right form or organization to do the job at hand. In the United States and certain European countries, many companies have divisional autonomy, but those that are international seldom apply this type of management to their subsidiaries abroad. As a result, they create massive communication problems for themselves.

This is reflected in a statement by C. F. Maxwell, formerly director of personnel of Courtaulds, Ltd.:

Communication is always difficult since it involves a number of departments and functions and a variety of recipients and subjects, such as employees, stockholders, technical matters, and company information. Whatever system or systems a company may have, there are invariably complaints about lack of communication and, on the other hand, about requests for, or supply of, unnecessary information.

It is very difficult to know the correct balance between centralization and decentralization for control and other purposes. Large companies appear to vary widely in their ideas on this subject, and, within each organization, patterns vary according to the circumstances at particular times. Consequently, there are wide variations in their interpretation of the basic information that is required....

In a multinational company whose *cheval de bataille* is a product of advanced technology, the director of technical support attributed the pains in communication between headquarters and subsidiaries to organizational schemes tailored to one market and expanded internationally without significant adjustments. The director said that he believes most communication failures result from unawareness of, or unwillingness or inability to observe, the maxim that international organizational arrangements should be tailored around the shortest lines of communication. Other experienced executive agreed and cited a number of examples documenting the wisdom of following the shortest lines of communication. Said one vice president:

Getting technical information to the subsidiaries where it must be used is a very hard job in itself. This job is made that much harder and that much less efficient by our company's insistence on long lines of command. Such lines have worked very nicely in the domestic market, but they have failed in foreign markets.

Many international authorities said that at this stage matters relating to organizational structure are very speculative and that books give no clues on how to handle them. Some senior executives stated the opinion that organizational approaches have failed in the past because management has not tried to maximize the comparative advantages of each approach or has failed to give major differences in organizational needs the perspective they deserve. Eberhard Schmidt provided an especially meaningful explanation:

Usually there is considerable difference between the legal and operational structures of a company. The legal structure must be designed to maintain sufficient control, especially from the financial standpoint, while taking into account local legislation and political conditions, and the need for freedom of action. The company's general aims are to optimize cash flow in both directions (repatriation of profits and investments from central sources), minimize taxes and currency losses, and maximize the security for the shareholders. A well-known example of the implementation of such policies was the influx of U.S. companies into Switzerland during the past ten years or so.

As to the operational organization structure, the main problem is how to establish the right relationships between central authority and operating groups; that is, to find the right balance between centralization and decentralization. This is an ever-present problem, even though there is only one sensible basic rule; namely, to centralize responsibility for strategic planning and control, and decentralize responsibility for local planning, operations, and profitability.

In a system of this kind there is a constant danger of either strong central power, causing a loss of initiative at the periphery, or lack of central authority, permitting centrifugal forces to become too strong. In the past most geographically decentralized organizations oscillated between these two extremes in cycles of 15 to 20 years' duration—excessive centralization followed by intense decentralization, followed by centralization. However, thanks to modern scientific management, information, and training, the amplitude and frequency of these oscillations are steadily diminishing.

With few exceptions, the point of view held by headquarters executives in international companies is that foreign subsidiaries are weak and need long-term guidance. If subsidiaries are fitted snugly into a worldwide organization, and carefully supervised when they are given operating authority, they should flourish. However, subsidiary executives are offended by excess supervision and resent being tapped on the back every 24 hours. They nourish the desire for more action among equals and for working more closely with other subsidiaries.

This point has been emphasized by M. Y. Yoshino, chairman of the international business and comparative management program, Graduate School of Business Administration, University of Southern California, Los Angeles, as follows:

Some firms choose to centralize practically all decision making at corporate headquarters and to require from foreign units extremely detailed operating plans and reports with great frequency. As one would expect, this arrangement tends to dampen the enthusiasm and initiative of the management overseas and to limit its flexibility and freedom in meeting local problems and opportunities.*

Headquarters executives invariably commented that overseas management is entitled to receive the same staff assistance as domestic divisions. They pointed out that

---

* M. Y. Yoshino, "Toward a Concept of Managerial Control for a World Enterprise," *Michigan Business Review,* March 1966.

lines of communication are open between overseas executives and top management at headquarters, and between departmental managers of overseas subsidiaries and departmental managers in the head office; therefore, specialized assistance should be no problem. The men abroad disagree and offer the following type of remark:

> The subsidiary or affiliate is usually small, while the corporation is big and sectioned. In most cases, there is little or no reflection of the subsidiary's image at headquarters and vice versa.

Not only do the parent companies and their foreign subsidiaries and affiliates differ in size and in departmentalization but also in organizational structure. Lack of data about structure is often synonymous with lack of clarity about who should send reports to whom. Organizational differences blur established communications channels, increase red tape, and reinforce informal channels.

The director of an American auditing firm operating in Guatemala spoke of the numerous communication problems he has encountered that are organizational in nature. In his opinion, U.S. companies are so well organized and their organizational lines so well observed that corporate executives can operate by the book, but in overseas subsidiaries the only executives who can succeed are those who improvise. And, since improvisation results in even greater departure from the guidelines, communication problems are aggravated rather than eased.

A corporate vice president remarked:

> It is amazing how many top-drawer managers don't know what goes on in their own organization. While part of the fault rests with the company, part of it is attributable to the individual himself.
>
> We all tend to use our own jargon. We find it prestigious to possess what others do not

have. And this is just as true of information and down-to-earth understanding as it is of property.

Admittedly, management thinking has gone through some violent upheavals in the past decade, but it will have to undergo further changes before such differences can be resolved.

Philippe Levi, general manager of Bull-General Electric's subsidiary in Mexico, said that he thinks international executives must give their immediate and "undivided" attention to two key responsibilities: (1) the drive for financial results and (2) the obligation for sales performance.

The two goals are not always complementary. They sometimes contradict each other, especially in advanced technological companies that rent rather than sell their products and that have equipment amortized by their subsidiaries. Such is the case with computers. The more computers a subsidiary places on the market on a rental basis, the more in the red it will be—until rental income exceeds the cost of replacements to the subsidiary. Since this situation is unlikely in a rapidly expanding market, it is no wonder that the subsidiary general manager suffers daily shocks as he faces choices of budgets versus sales. He may spend more time effecting compromises than following an aggressive marketing policy.

Many experienced men pointed out that it takes a long time to build the marketing side of a subsidiary, especially when competition is stiff and numerous handicaps must be overcome. But it takes a relatively brief period for a subsidiary to run down its share of the market as a result of budgetary controls that are too tight, lack of market studies, or other constraints and deficiencies. Depending on the objectives and policies of the parent company, overseas executives are faced with a choice of maintaining budgetary standards or capturing a bigger share of the market. The decision is often complex because of the numerous factors involved.

The rather consistent failure of companies to establish the right functional balance stems in part from organizational discrepancies between headquarters and subsidiaries. Several general managers of subsidiaries said that their burden would be eased tremendously if somebody at headquarters had to live under the same stress; that is, had to make a choice between financial and sales considerations, but this seldom occurs.

The international vice president may face some problems of this type if he is directly responsible for both sales and financial performance. But this study disclosed few such cases; in most of them the area directors had only marketing responsibility, and the area controller ran the controllership offices on his own. And it is unlikely that the area controllers had any concern about meeting sales quotas.

There is evidence that having a triumvirate share the burden eases some problems, although it creates others. The triumvirate consists of the general manager of a subsidiary and his marketing and finance directors. However, not all problems can be handled by this group. Major problems have to be referred to headquarters for a decision.

Over a period of time, excessive control by headquarters compounds these problems and erects, rather than eases, communication barriers. At this point, foreign experience is essential. No matter how intelligent a man is, he cannot understand conditions in a foreign country if he has not been exposed to them. This was emphasized by the director of finance of an American company abroad; his extensive experience in various business environments made him exceptionally qualified to diagnose causes and to suggest remedies for communication ailments:

I know the foreign countries to which I have been assigned quite well, as do the men with whom I work. When we in the subsidiary recommend something, our recommendation is based on our cool estimate of the local facts as we see them. How the headquarters, which is thousands of miles away, can reverse strong recommendations by subsidiary management puzzles me. If the foreign executive is wrong . . . he should be fired; if he is not, his recommendations should be followed. He can then be judged on the results he obtains.

Executive Availability, Ability, and Experience

When Ford Motor Company began its Mexican operations in 1963 and 1964, top management sent down a team of approximately a hundred key men from the United States. Three years later, the team was reduced to 50, and plans were made to transfer still other men back to the United States and replace them with local management. The replacement of foreign management with local management occurred at the same time that employment increased from three thousand men to four thousand.

The use of local staff is highly desirable, and it is becoming increasingly popular among international companies. However, the change from foreign to local executives evidently poses substantial problems. For one thing, subsidiary executives need an opportunity to learn and grow by taking risks and making their own mistakes, but few companies are willing to give them the necessary freedom. Second, the development and training of local men can be costly.

Some foreign executives in Latin America commented that the issue there is not the cost involved in setting up an able training program but the loss of qualified personnel they are experiencing afterward. Said a senior executive in Mexico: "Our experience has been that after we train a man he moves to another American company, and with this he gets a 30 percent, and sometimes even a 40 percent, increase in his salary. Mobility is occurring here in a big way."

Participating executives estimated that over two-thirds of the international communication difficulties experienced by their companies are caused by men who are oriented to a product line that is being phased out. These men have never undergone internal training and have not been exposed to the highly varied environments in which the companies must now operate.

A manufacturer of technological products expressed the opinion that executive development has been slow to gain acceptance because most of the men currently running companies never participated in formal executive development programs and cannot grasp the need for them. These executives do not realize the extent to which programs can ease a company's multinational communication problems.

Particularly concerned about poor communication were the managers who had extensive experience in operations outside their country of origin and those who had spent a substantial part of their business careers abroad. These men referred to two major causes of communication problems:

- The top executives in the corporate organization who are assigned to run the international operations lack multinational experience. At best, these men have traveled extensively, but they have not taken grass-roots assignments abroad.
- Few companies, even those with more than half of their business abroad, have enough experienced international executives on their boards of directors.

Other participants agreed that many international management problems can be attributed to the lack of international experience at top echelons. The managing director of a subsidiary commented:

The particular problems we face in this country can be understood by a man who has been abroad on an assignment for five or more years. But they cannot be understood by a man whose entire career has been in his country of origin.

And another international executive complained:

Headquarters is always telling us that they have found this or that practice very sound in our 80 offices in the United States, and asking, "Why wouldn't it be a sound practice in Mexico?" Our reply that Mexico is not the United States never seems to ring any bells.

That extensive red tape does not guarantee efficiency also does not seem to ring any bells. Thomas McDonald, of Price Waterhouse in Mexico, remarked that, if a man does not know immediately what he is trying to control, it is only human for him to request much more information than he really needs. Much of the red tape crowding the desks of international executives results from lack of international experience at headquarters. Although it seems illogical for one to write about things without having some basic knowledge about them, there is plenty of evidence that the practice is common in the international field.

The author asked the general manager of a major subsidiary, who had previously served as area director, what he would do if he returned to his old job, now that he had subsidiary experience. His reply was that his current experience helped open his eyes to a number of things that looked trivial from a distance but in reality were quite important.

Some participants emphasized that international executives need to be particularly

sensitive to environmental factors. Dan Tol-
kowsky, president of Israel's Discount Bank
Investment Corporation, stated:

> Other than having been at the "receiving
> end" of quite a few executives from abroad,
> we have little experience in evaluating ex-
> ecutives, but it seems to me that the crux of
> the issue lies in the personal leadership qual-
> ities of the individual expert. Of course,
> above all else this implies understanding
> and persuasiveness in a foreign environment.
> These I have often found woefully lacking.

That there are differences in conditions,
practices, and skills in various countries is
common knowledge among mature international executives, particularly those who
have been exposed to many different environments abroad. They make comparisons
and draw their own conclusions. But these
differences are not known by many executives at headquarters; so their conclusions
may be erroneous.

Frustrated communication efforts—especially regarding financial matters—could
easily bring about disenchantment in many
echelons of multinational companies. Yet
no such mood was evident in the companies
that were visited in the course of this study.
Nonetheless, top management still needs to
expose headquarters executives to the challenges of their field operations.

Top management should not assume that
this will happen automatically, nor should
it expect executives abroad to season their
counterparts in the home office through correspondence and informal chats. Even when
this does happen, the results are usually far
from effective. A subsidiary general manager
experiencing this type of situation said:

> What headquarters is asking us to do would
> eventually result in our spending most of
> our time communicating. But our product
> line is such that overcommunication, like
> overcontrol, would not allow us to do an

honest job abroad. If I were to do everything
I am told to do by the home office, I would
be snowed down throughout the year.

> One needs some freedom. Besides, I believe
> that if a company places a manager on top
> of a subsidiary, it does so because it trusts
> him. And if the company trusts him it
> should do so all the way and judge his per-
> formance on only end results.

Local Technical
and Professional Skills

Throughout certain parts of the
world, the lack of skilled personnel is a per-
sistent problem. Domestic and international
companies alike are plagued by inability
to find trained people. Moreover, companies
can never assume that people who seem
qualified can actually administer a function
or an activity. As one overseas financial director exclaimed: "In this country 'CPA'
doesn't mean a damn. I would rather hire a
high school graduate who passes our basic
accounting test than a university graduate
who flops it."

In several countries, university education
was severely attacked by both local and foreign executives. A major criticism was that
political activities consume too much of
students' time and energy. Another complaint was that teaching is little more than
pumping things into people's heads. Students do not learn how to think and consequently are unable to communicate well.
Clear-eyed headquarters executives who
have made an effort to study the problem
have come to the same conclusion.

The lack of technical skills is a serious hin-
drance to a country's industrial development, which in turn can have serious political and social repercussions. And the chain
reaction continues: Unless a country's political situation is sound, neither educational
nor economic development can take place.

The misfortune of one country may turn out to be a gift to its neighbors. Because of Guatemala's political instability in 1967, several companies sought investment opportunities in neighboring countries that were members of the Central American Common Market.

Local personnel, particularly accountants, play a vital role in communication. When a company operates on a profit-and-loss basis, its need for top accountants is critical since headquarters must rely on them for careful cost analyses and accurate, timely reports.

No doubt, many corporations hope that their subsidiaries can either find or train good men, but they forget about local conditions. All foreign companies operating in Guatemala, for example, find it difficult to obtain the services of well-trained accountants. The accountants they do hire always seem to vanish immediately after being trained. Thus international accountants are obliged to do more than the traditional auditing and consulting functions. One of their new functions is hiring and training personnel. Some companies try to recruit skilled men from other countries—Mexico and Venezuela being two main sources—and even canvas Europe, where Switzerland has been a good source.

The difficulty in obtaining dependable accountants locally is particularly regrettable since, as previously mentioned, a company relies heavily on their reports and since its information system often follows the pattern of its accounting system. The collection of reliable information on a country-by-country basis and its classification into appropriate groups could provide top management with a new perspective on overseas operations. However, this is seldom possible; so corporate plans are made on the basis of far more rudimentary data.

Clumsy information gathering, invalid analysis of data, erroneous evaluation of performance, and inaccurate estimates of profit and loss—all reduce to a minimum the challenges experienced by the local managers and their feeling of contribution to the company as a whole. Often, the result is further limitations on initiative and freedom of action, and further distortions of procedures. At that point, assigned tasks no longer stimulate productive action.

This situation seems to prevail throughout Central America and in several South American countries. Unquestionably, it affects communication with headquarters—a problem that the foreign executive has to explain, defend, and eventually solve. Very few countries have the technical skills they require for two basic reasons: Their technology is only recently imported, and their higher educational systems are not yet geared to produce engineers and technicians. They are also not yet geared to produce managers.

American companies are by no means the only ones handicapped by this lack of local skills. An Italian manufacturer of precision and business equipment found that the standard of technicians and specialized workers it employed in Mexico was below expected levels. The main reason seemed to be that Mexican workers were not accustomed to precision technology. As a remedial measure, the company established a training school for specialized workers. According to the school's director, if Mexican technicians receive adequate training, they can reach about 70 percent of the standard performance of technicians in highly industrialized countries.

Even if a subsidiary has a versatile engineering staff, redesign considerations are always part of the picture. Differences in metric systems and standards make redesign considerations mandatory, as do three other factors:

- Locally manufactured parts that do not follow original specifications.
- Differences in the materials to be used.
- Differences in the machinery available, and in the standards and performance of the equipment.

Because these factors cause delays that hurt sales, the marketing director usually revolts. They also result in added costs, which prompts the finance director to complain. The snag is that the man most involved, the engineering director, is seldom part of the key management group.

Some European manufacturers expressed the opinion that the equipment used in their operations in Mexico, and more par-

ticularly the equipment used by their suppliers, is fairly obsolete when compared with that used in their own countries and that this affects the level of skills available. A senior manager of an Italian company explained the situation:

Industry in Italy has a long tradition. But it began in Latin America only after the second World War. Argentina was first; it now has almost 20 years' experience in precision manufacturing. However, Mexico has only five years of steady effort along the same line. Hence it is no wonder that our Argentinian engineers and specialized workers are better than those who are Mexican, and our Italian specialists are doing even better than those in the other two operations.

6. Solutions: Management, Media, and Men

COMPANIES THAT MANAGE their operations from a distance require two basic factors: effective management methods and able executives. That these needs are recognized was confirmed by numerous executives who participated in this study. Some of them reported difficulties and made suggestions; others described methods by which their companies had overcome communication barriers.

Of the many suggestions offered by international executives, the following seemed most incisive and representative:

- The international company, instead of trying to control every detail of world-wide operations, should set objectives and base evaluation on performance in reaching these objectives. Both factors are important, both influence communication, and both affect the acquisition and retention of able executives.
- To increase the sensitivity of headquarters men to foreign conditions, it should be mandatory that managerial positions at the international division be filled with executives who have experience abroad.
- Acquiring broader knowledge of the situation in which each subsidiary operates is certainly a very good step toward the possibility of better communication.
- International companies should invite subsidiary managers to attend courses or other planned meetings at headquarters lasting several days at a time so that managers can meet their counterparts around the world and develop a common base of thought, principles, and aims.

Many suggestions made by executives were broad in scope, as were a number of the programs described by companies that had been unsuccessful in their attempts to solve communication problems. By contrast, many attempts that had some degree of success were specific, concrete programs or methods, such as the following, summarized by a participating executive:

We attempt to overcome communication barriers by providing guidelines, using telex and telephone, and emphasizing communication problems in management schools.

Organizational Considerations

When a general manager of a foreign subsidiary does exchange information with headquarters, one of their first concerns is business opportunity. In many companies, headquarters has—as it should—a knowledgeable staff to provide such information. Assessment of opportunities abroad, and of the way they have been handled, are far more important than the flow of paper and the money paid for cables. A chief executive officer aptly remarked:

The assessment of opportunity for future progress is our foremost preoccupation. This is consistent with the company's basic approach to managing its international business, which includes an experienced group of international specialists at headquarters, business intelligence offices staffed for complete and accurate service in certain overseas centers, market research offices at a number of other points of business concentration, participation in economic and financial research institutions, close working relationships with leading local banks in every commercially important foreign city where the company has operations, coordination of the full range of worldwide services, and prompt information to our senior staffs in overseas operations regarding all developments affecting their work.

International companies need communications systems that can be adapted to changes in requirements and demands. A great degree of organizational flexibility, for instance, is required to take advantage of the constant changes in the taxation and tariff structures of different nations and to exploit new growth opportunities. This cannot be accomplished by remote control.

One solution is to have two types of communication: one for all international subsidiaries that conforms to a pre-established pattern and one that is more flexible and varies from country to country. This variation is needed to reflect the particular conditions, legal as well as operational, present in a particular country and therefore requires a thorough examination of the conditions and opportunities characteristic of the country.

A computer manufacturer's efforts to disseminate information on a worldwide scale were constantly hampered by delays, even when there were no identifiable reasons. The company finally set up a separate department to handle communications and provide information guidance. A senior executive, commenting on the compatibility of the new arrangement with standard organizational procedures, remarked:

What we come up with as a solution often depends on the problem we are facing. It may be a crash program or a product extremely difficult to handle. This calls for approaches to communications that are atypical and unusual.

Thus, subsequent to our crash program, we began building a technical marketing organization to accompany the development of the applications field. We know that unless this is done, future markets may slip out of our hands.

To help ease the communication barrier, another international company reorganized its regional coordination function, so that it was half geographic and half product, rather than completely geographic. The regional directors and their assistants were situated in New York, but spent half their time abroad.

However, marketing problems are not the only ones requiring fast and reliable communications linkages. Engineering is another critical function. Labor negotiations around the world are just as vital and difficult, and top management must keep informed about other important activities. These often require telephone and interphone usage.

Organizational considerations involve not only what is written in company manuals but also executives' personalities. A strong personality often changes priorities of established practices and modifies the gray areas of policies so that they conform with his own thinking. A general manager remarked: "I get a little confused about line and staff. In international industrial operations, things simply don't work the way the books say they do." The end result is that key men spend time around a table attempting to sort these things out.

Many companies advocate the division of responsibilities and have very sound reasons for doing so. Companies that place the area controllership directly under the wing of the financial vice president, and completely outside international operations, provide excellent reasons for justifying their choice. Finance is no longer an accounting-oriented function; it now includes financial planning, budgets, and control. As such, it must be forward-looking and able to work independently of operations.

Some companies consider it unwise to assign a manager the control over his actions and the subsequent evaluation of his own performance. Other companies believe that managers should be almost totally responsible for their own operations. The fact that both approaches are right for some organizations does not make the manager's stress less real. But it does mean that efforts should be made to develop efficient solutions—even if such solutions are actually a compromise.

Switching functions among key executives offers an excellent alternative to reorganization, since communication barriers are often a state of mind. The financial man is constantly characterized by operating executives as being farther away from the product and the market than any other man in the organization. As one operating vice president pointed out:

> Financial men may be experts in financial matters, but often, too often, they lack sensitivity about products and sales. Financial procedures are not yet tooled to face the behavior of a dynamic market. A good deal of time goes into doing, undoing, redoing, and reviewing financial plans. Such activities consume too much precious time of my people abroad.

This is strong language. Directors of finance reacted to this thought by saying that many changes in financial plans and procedures are not their doing but are the reflection of marketing policy changes over which they really have no control. Commented the director of finance of a multinational enterprise:

> It is a fact that over the past year we had too many policy changes, but the very large majority of them resulted from operational considerations and originated outside my sphere.

Other executives said that, in so new a field as international industrial management, changes are necessary to correct deficiencies and to steer away from inefficient courses. And some men added that changes are necessary to shake the international enterprise and its executives to their complacent cores. The alternative is that international companies pay a more expensive ticket in terms of stagnation.

Developing Multidimensional Approaches

Senior executives in 17 countries emphasized their wish to see efficient solutions implemented soon. Otherwise, they fear, they will continue to get the worst of all worlds; and, even less desirable, they will probably suffer relative deterioration in the standards of their communications. At this point, improvements in just one sector are not enough; they must be multidimensional if they are to be effective.

Underlying the various suggestions was the recurring idea that international companies need to develop a program that will provide "the sort of key information needed" so that substantial decision making will be left to the local operating level. The men who provided the most glowing testimonials on this topic emphasized that communication problems, and the data burden, are often an aftermath of headquarters' drive to lower the level of decisions that can be made by local executives.

METHODS

Whatever media are used to solve particular communication problems, the important thing is to insure that the undertaking is deliberate, not haphazard. When general managers of subsidiaries meet headquarters executives, each of them should be given a chance to explain and identify his objectives and his problems. They should be encouraged to describe stumbling blocks—political, social, or operational—that have affected their short-term and long-term goals and other critical issues.

Much attention should be given to the executives' specific needs. They usually require and want a full explanation of the company's organizational structure and activities. Executives really interested in efficiency want only key information. Anything else is a waste of their time.

The general manager of an American subsidiary in Mexico found an efficient way to reduce his communication burden. He analyzed the information in the reports headquarters was asking him to submit and found that most of it could easily be collected at headquarters, thus easing the load of paper going through the pipeline. Using headquarters' big computer as the pivot point, the general manager suggested, and obtained agreement, that all his important data be forwarded to the home office and kept there. The results showed promise of a communication breakthrough.

In the opinion of overseas operating executives, headquarters should collect, intelligently filter, and disseminate information that is accurate, timely, and significant to the subsidiary's business. This is especially essential today since too often the communication pipeline is clogged with irrelevant information. Overseas executives also complained that some data from headquarters are not cross-validated and are crowded with myths.

One international executive commented: "Poor communications are usually the result of inability to write clearly, combined with the writer's lack of forethought or his failure to put himself in the position of the recipient." Thus the message is as important as the medium, and improvement of

only one of them is not enough to remove a barrier.

An executive of a leading financial institution pointed out that its communications from subsidiaries involve much more than administrative matters. The overseas subsidiaries channel to headquarters timely information on general conditions, political developments, economic opportunities, important visitors (whose presence may have an impact on development), and new ventures.

The design of an efficient communications system can be seen as a process in which a goal is set, data are collected, and a decision is made on priorities. In many firms, the goals of international corporate communication should be to establish procedures that will improve the transmission and processing of information, to use methods that are clear to all concerned, and to bring procedures, methods, and practices in line with modern thinking. The average executive should be able to grasp the broad outlines of his communication rights and obligations in one comprehensive policy.

All aspects of the communications system need to be as simple and complete as possible. This is essential to avoid misunderstandings. Also, every effort should be made to coordinate such communications to make the executive's job more effective. This takes more doing than saying, particularly when a company honestly wants solutions that will benefit all parties to the communication.

Effective information flow minimizes variations in reporting and reduces misinterpretation, though it does not eliminate the need for more immediate and more personal communications such as visits and telephone calls. International subsidiaries usually require a multidimensional approach that is appropriate for their operations. Therefore, methods workable at home are sometimes more disadvantageous than advantageous. It is neither necessary nor effective to make the international communications network follow the pattern of the headquarters network.

Media

An American electronics company encountered growing pains in the financial control of its Mexican operations because of unprecedented business growth. To improve the situation, the company established a worldwide financial plan and set up standardized control. But it found that applying the same standards everywhere was difficult, while flexibility in standards seemed to cause increased variation among the countries, Mexico being only one example.

The company finally developed a form to ease the serialization of financial data through telegraph and telex. Its approach was similar to that used on classic tabulating equipment, with some modifications for telex transmission. Thus the code permitted improved communication with the other Latin American operations of the corporation—a must since airmail letters took ten to fifteen days to reach São Paulo and telephone communications had almost prohibitive delays.

Several companies abroad now send their correspondence by air package, which is delivered to the airport, put into the pilot's hands, and picked up from him at the destination. Fans of Western movies recognize this as a process dating back to horse-and-buggy days.

One condition that creates one-dimensional solutions is relying too much on a single medium. One executive said: "It is our opinion that in this age of communication there are very few barriers to good communication with the field. Telephone, cables, and airmail have reduced all of the

old barriers." However, other executives pointed out that in some countries these services still have severe limitations.

To get out of the communications squeeze, many companies use several media. One firm sends urgent reports by air package from airport to airport and has also installed a private radio network that links the seven branches with the subsidiary's headquarters and factory. The director of finance commented: "We find it of invaluable assistance. It costs, but is worth it."

There is no doubt that companies need some imaginative solutions, even if they are costly on the surface. An international financial institution established the policy that, when a problem proves too difficult to discuss by letter or phone, the executive abroad is to be invited to fly to headquarters with all the documents. This organization also tried to insure that every subsidiary abroad would be visited at least once annually by an officer with the authority, ability, and time to sit down and talk. "Even so," said the vice president who was interviewed, "communication is our biggest problem, and we constantly look for ways of improving it."

Roland Grassberger, of Honeywell Venezuela, offered several solutions to communication problems. One was that regional meetings should be beefed up and should include not only the first layer but also the second layer of an organization. To this, he added that both layers should meet at least once a year. He said that such meetings are much more important in Latin America than in Europe because of deficiencies in the mechanical aspects of communication, primarily the slow mail deliveries and hard-to-get telephones. He conceded that personal meetings are more expensive, but so is the use of some communications media. Telex, for example, costs up to five times more in Latin America than it does in Europe on a package-deal basis.

The general manager of a subsidiary in Central America was most emphatic in stating his opinion that increasing personal contact on a two-way basis would contribute significantly to easing communication barriers and establishing feedback. His thesis was that "close personal contact" should, but seldom does, work two ways. In his experience most visits of headquarters executives are "superficial."

Many heads of subsidiaries or divisions overseas doubted that fairly unilateral direction from corporate headquarters can provide the right mixture of freedom and firmness that is needed. They favored—and would like to promote—a get-together of subsidiary managers. Some senior directors believe that companies should organize worldwide meetings for key personnel in which emphasis is placed on identifying and solving communication problems. Executives who had used, or who wanted to use, this approach said that, although such meetings are costly, they are beneficial because they help the subsidiary general manager understand how his colleagues work, what kinds of problems other executives face, and what solutions have been found to solve these problems.

An executive of a company manufacturing precision equipment remarked:

We need dynamic international management able to turn stones over and find out what lies under them. To mention just one of our problems, we asked area management for certain equipment items and were told that none of the countries in the area had a surplus of the items we needed.

The fact was that some of them were loaded with idle equipment, while we were equipment-hungry. But because we communicated with area management only, we had no way to find out what was available.

This situation was finally resolved by direct talks of the subsidiaries' general managers with one another—rather than with headquarters or area management.

That blockage of this magnitude occurs prompted a key executive of a participating company to remark that "someone's priorities have gone rather queer."

The fact is that aims and priorities of individuals or groups laboring in different environments must be *expected* to diverge. A production group and a marketing group will ordinarily come up with different ideas of what constitutes success. Each has a life of its own and seeks to preserve, define, and perpetuate itself even at the expense of the interests of the company as a whole. Each can be expected to hoard human and physical assets and to play down (if not suppress) news unfavorable to itself. This is natural human behavior observed every day even in specialized groups situated in the same city. The tendency explodes in magnitude when distance cuts down on the chances to exchange views, study problems together, understand obstacles, and work out aims together.

The binding thread of much good communication between international executives needs to be an exchange of facts and thinking and guidelines directed toward making the actions of one man (or a unit in one country) predictable and understandable to another. Many an angry radiogram is sent because the decision of one executive is a shock to someone who feels that a contrary decision on the same set of facts should have been "obvious." Building up a common body of knowledge, shared aims, and shared ideas about the measurement of success is important in minimizing these surprises.

Although international executives busy themselves with the search for solutions to their communication problems, they find that solutions do not come easily. Prescriptions for the treatment of communication ills cannot be impersonal, nor can they be administered routinely. Research on communication should include some study of differences existing from country to country and from area to area. Professor Eberhard Schmidt, general manager of the German Brown Bovari Company, summed up the situation as follows:

> One of the most difficult problems in a multinational enterprise is to decide who should know what and in what form it should be communicated. . . .
>
> There is no doubt that delegation is one of the first conditions for simplifying communication; but, even so, reporting in all forms is unavoidable, as is rapid communication in case of emergencies. Frequent personal contacts are undoubtedly highly important and more useful than any amount of written inquiries and explanations, and for this reason executives of international companies must be willing and able to do a considerable amount of traveling.
>
> In my opinion, not one international company has so far been able to solve the communication problem in an entirely satisfactory way. . . .

Developing Effective Communicators

Communication barriers cannot be overcome unless the men concerned view their responsibilities within a broad framework.

Regional executives argue that present communication problems will be eased only when the men at headquarters "develop a better understanding of international business and learn the fundamentals of industrial operations in individual countries." They suggest that this working knowledge should include general aspects of business abroad and personal experience with at least one of the functional areas, such as production, marketing, or finance.

Headquarters executives argue that pres-

ent problems will be eased only when executives in the field "develop a better understanding of international business and take a more global view of problems and business opportunities." They suggest that executives in any one country need to give more consideration to the effect of their requests for capital and their production and marketing plans on the operations of the company as a whole. They maintain that division and subsidiary executives often "suboptimize"—that is, they take action favorable for their own units but not in the best interests of an efficient worldwide operation.

A big factor in breaking down insularity is the growing willingness of executives to try to understand communication problems. This presupposes an orientation that is broad, contemporary, and participative. Successful multinational operations are based on a team effort. But the broadminded approach also requires a thorough knowledge of the contribution that each function can make to the total business effort. Being interested in the activities of others is natural; most executives are concerned whether other departments have more status, staff, and resources than their own.

An important factor in overcoming communication problems is recognizing that the masses of paper and red tape must be scaled down. Selectivity in what is transmitted helps; but, like filtering, selectivity is subjective. Even more important is the climate or spirit within the company regarding communication. Although one would expect a favorable climate to exist in any dynamic company, it cannot be taken for granted.

STAFFING

An important axiom regarding effective international communications is that they require experienced communicators—men who are experienced and knowledgeable about the subjects to be communicated and skilled in the communication process. Though many companies have first-class executives in their foreign offices, few have enough competent executives to meet future turnover, promotion, and expansion.

How many executives should a company have in its inventory? At present, the only way to determine this is by studying what has been successfully done in domestic operations and then apply it to the worldwide situation. Frederick G. Donner, former General Motors board chairman and chief executive officer, is quoted as having said: "We try to keep a manpower pool which is a bit more than twice as large as the number of jobs which it will fill." Because of GM overseas operations' market expansion, depth in management is especially important.

The Bank of America hoped to ease its international communication burden and overcome bottlenecks by being more selective in its acquisition of key personnel. It began hiring more men with master's and doctorate degrees; the rationale was that, other things being equal, the company would have greater potential. J. Gallo, assistant vice president, international, remarked:

> Because most men can get a bachelor's degree these days, the population of bachelor-degree holders increases steadily. But it takes more time and effort to get an MBA, and still more for a PhD. The men coming out of postgraduate university programs are mature, and we can see to it that they get a better part of themselves involved in their work when we send them abroad.

Many men now in the international field were recruited on university campuses; then, soon after they were hired, they took a company training program. This program,

with its courses and some minor job assignments, usually lasted from eight to ten months. During this time, the future executive may be tested to determine his abilities, aptitudes, and interests. In some cases, his ability to communicate is also tested. Obviously, companies do not want to rely solely on comfortable assumptions that university graduates will be able to handle all types of situations and problems.

One American company strengthened its working relationship with executives assigned abroad by staffing its international headquarters with men who had international experience. In addition, 70 percent of the international division's senior management consisted of former general managers of subsidiaries abroad, and the company planned to eventually increase this ratio to 100 percent. Also included on this staff were a number of foreign nationals—men from the various countries and areas of the world where the company does business—and experts in trade financing, money markets, and international labor. Another commendable practice of this company was that its headquarters officers traveled extensively in the countries within their assigned areas. As a result of these practices, the company developed a very strong working relationship with its overseas executives.

The Bank of America described the exchanges of executives between its national and international operations. Significantly, said J. Gallo, the impetus came from the national organization—it felt the need to enrich its ranks with international experience before the international executives expressed a desire for domestic experience.

International companies need all-round men capable of responding intelligently to an ever changing world. Small companies engaged in international operations seem to be especially aware that people assigned abroad must be more versatile than their domestic counterparts. Nils J. Ledertoug, administrative sales manager of American Motors International, remarked: "These men must be able to change hats in two seconds. They must be more technically oriented and at the same time more marketing- and advertising-oriented." Other executives who were interviewed emphasized that smaller companies need this versatility because they cannot afford the multilayer specialization characteristic of big industrial combines.

When men who are versatile—or *polyvalant* as the French call them—are given assignments abroad, their companies usually anticipate an improvement in performance and greater penetration of foreign markets. These expectations help to create improvements in communication, which, in turn, provide a climate conducive to success.

TRAINING

Communication can be improved tremendously by appropriate training. The benefits are multiple, ranging from reducing the need for communication to better interpretation of semantic meaning, and from that to more effective usage of mechanics.

In one participating company, all managers working abroad—American and foreign personnel alike—are trained at headquarters. The executive participating in this study commented proudly: "Most officers overseas are the product of our own training school." He confirmed that the training had eased the company's communication problems.

The Bank of America has been very conscious of the need for good communication and carefully observes the development of these skills from the beginning of a man's career.

Early in its training programs, the bank makes a point of keeping communications channels open and letting the men in train-

ing know that they can depend on headquarters for support. About six years ago, the bank conducted a study and found that communication problems were contributing to its high attrition rate. One of the remedial steps taken by the bank was to establish a policy that executives would not be censored for making decisions, only for not making them. The policy, it must be added, specifies that, when an overseas executive makes a decision, he must be ready to back it up by documenting it himself.

Mature foreign executives support the thesis that they are better off when they stand up for their opinions from the very beginning rather than accepting the role of a yes man until they learn. Said George W. Teague, general manager of Guatemala's Tipic:

> When I present sound arguments, top management listens to what I say. But a junior executive assigned abroad has to speak firmly and soundly from the very beginning of his career. He has to understand that he cannot accept the colors of a yes man for a time, and then decide to become authoritative.

Some companies follow another approach: concentrating on the almost impossible job of internal personnel relations. They have assigned key people the task of carrying geniality and goodwill to all areas, in the course of which they take a long, hard look.

In general, participants agreed that all educational programs designed for international executives should emphasize communication and avoid overspecialization. Because international executives need an understanding of cultural and historical forces that mold society, a broad education is preferable to a narrow one. However, once an executive is given an overseas assignment, he needs some specialized courses in languages and customs.

P. T. Welborn, treasurer, Goodyear de

Venezuela, who attended the American Institute of Foreign Trade prior to his first foreign assignment in Peru, dramatized this point when he commented that the AIFT program enabled him to adjust to the environment he encountered in the foreign assignment:

> Basically, you have to be adaptable as hell overseas. At AIFT, I learned things that none of us learned academically. Also I found that the social life that goes on at the school is good experience for subsequent assignment abroad.

Hopes of overcoming communication barriers in international industrial operations will continue to be relegated to dreamland if companies persist in disassociating communication from the management to be served. Moreover, companies cannot derive full benefit from their executive and manpower resources unless they make an effort to track down the paper tigers of communication.

In the years ahead, international enterprises should try hard to develop efficient communications systems. This calls for deeper study of the framework and methodology required for good information processing. It also calls for companies to go one step further and evolve fresh communications channels that will enable them to meet present and future needs.

For your interest
**Other Books on International Business
from the AMA Management Bookshelf**

Developing the International Executive

Dimitris N. Chorafas

Over 200 top managers throughout the world have been interviewed to provide these up-to-date facts on executive development as it is carried on in the field. The author explains what companies are doing to solve such problems as the communication gap between home and foreign office, job rotation of overseas personnel, development of national and third-country executives, and the lack of information on customs and regulations in foreign countries.
$7.50/AMA members: $5.00

Doing Business in and with Japan

Examines the intricacies of conducting business in and with Japan. The structure of the Japanese economy, including the influence of the Japanese government, is outlined. Factors in setting up a joint venture are presented as well as selection of a Japanese partner, marketing opportunities, and the effect of employment and compensation policies on business operations.
$6.00/AMA members: $4.00

Doing Business in Latin America

Edited by Thomas A. Gannon

Provides practical information on current Latin American business conditions for those businessmen who may be considering expansion into this market and for those who need specific information on operating problems.
$4.50/AMA members: $3.00

Financing East-West Business Transactions

Edited by John H. Hickman

Explores the financing and structure of trade between Eastern European countries and the West. Emphasizes various forms that the East-West transactions can take, gives specific examples, and indicates opportunities for increased trade with Eastern countries.
$4.50/AMA members: $3.00

The International Business Environment

A Management Guide

Harold J. Heck

Discusses the commercial policy framework of imports and exports, preferential trading agreements, restrictive practices in international business, tax considerations in foreign business, and the workings of international finance. Appendixes provide sources of international business intelligence and information on statistical systems and publications.
$6.75/AMA members: $4.50

Purchasing in Worldwide Operations

Robert Douglass Stuart

Using case studies, this bulletin pinpoints successful methods of purchasing from overseas suppliers and discusses the pros and cons of such operations.
$3.00/AMA members: $2.00

Researching the European Markets

Robert J. Alsegg

New insights into both market and marketing differences, based on interviews conducted in twelve different countries. These interviews included eighty industrial companies, thirty-four market research agencies, and fifteen other organizations. Emphasis is placed on consumer habits and national and industrial characteristics.
$12.00/AMA members: $8.00

Sourcebook of International Insurance and Employee Benefit Management

Volume 1: Europe

Carole S. Hart

This first of two volumes contains listings of information sources for European countries and 14 "briefs" on the corporate insurance and employee benefit situations in seven of these countries. The "briefs" were written by prominent European insurance men.
$10.50/AMA members: $7.00

Sourcebook on International Corporate Insurance and Employee Benefit Management

Volume 11: Selected Countries of the World

Robert Wells

Covers corporate insurance and employee benefit practices in 79 countries that are not, for the most part, highly industrialized or technologically advanced. "Country briefs" on 13 nations and "Area Briefs" on Asia, the Middle East, and Central America provide the background material to help develop and execute programs that will not conflict with foreign regulations or customs.
$15.00/AMA members: $10.00

Tax Considerations in Organizing Foreign Operations

Paul D. Seghers

Considers the burden of U.S. income tax restrictions on U.S. owners of firms that derive their income from overseas sources and shows the effect of these restrictions on the choice of corporate forms and methods of doing business abroad.
$3.00/AMA members: $2.00

If you would like to place an order, write to:
American Management Association, Inc.
135 West 50th Street
New York, N.Y. 10020

The Communication Barrier in International Management

Dimitris N. Chorafas

Many problems encountered by international companies stem from the communication barrier between headquarters and overseas subsidiaries. This problem persists despite companies' growing sophistication about international affairs and the reduction in time and money needed to span geographical distances. This study was conducted to find out why this communication weakness exists and how management can overcome it.

The author examines the following questions:

- Which executives are involved in the communication process?
- What kinds of information do they communicate?
- By what methods and how often do they communicate?
- What problems do companies have in maintaining communication between headquarters and their foreign subsidiaries?
- How can these problems be alleviated?
- What specific steps are companies taking to improve their communication?

The report is based on interviews with 106 company executives and 42 bankers, consultants, professors, and government and university administrators. Approximately 40 percent of the interviews were conducted in the United States; 30 percent in Europe; and 30 percent in Mexico, Central America, and Venezuela.

The author

Dimitris N. Chorafas has had a private management consulting practice in Paris since 1961. Prior to this he was affiliated with Booz, Allen and Hamilton International, Inc., as a director, management information systems. Dr. Chorafas is the author of 30 books and numerous articles on industrial research, engineering, applied mathematics, electronic computers, and management.

American Management Association, Inc.
135 West 50th Street
New York, New York 10020